Paper German

Paper German

A Political Policy Memoir

Peter Omoregbe

PAPER GERMAN
A POLITICAL POLICY MEMOIR

iUniverse books may be ordered through booksellers or by contacting:

iUniverse
1663 Liberty Drive
Bloomington, IN 47403
www.iuniverse.com
1-800-Authors (1-800-288-4677)

Because of the dynamic nature of the Internet, any web addresses or links contained in this book may have changed since publication and may no longer be valid. The views expressed in this work are solely those of the author and do not necessarily reflect the views of the publisher, and the publisher hereby disclaims any responsibility for them.

Any people depicted in stock imagery provided by Thinkstock are models, and such images are being used for illustrative purposes only. Certain stock imagery © Thinkstock.

ISBN: 978-1-5320-0601-2 (sc)
ISBN: 978-1-5320-0602-9 (e)

Library of Congress Control Number: 2016915053

Print information available on the last page.

iUniverse rev. date: 10/18/2016

Contents

Introduction

PAPER GERMAN IS ABOUT THE denials that nonethnic Germans living in Germany face on a systematic basis. This trend is not just limited to the older generations of migrants who have settled in Germany; it also affects their children. Migrants living in Germany are consumed by the flames of denial in everyday life. They keep wondering whether they haven't done enough to improve their lives. They keep hoping for better days, but time is limited.

Here is a compilation that details the experiences I've had living here in Germany.

***

Don't "black" me, because you don't know me. Don't black me, because I know you don't know me.

Don't black me. Like you, I am on earth.

Don't black me. When I am no more, the same destiny will shape you. Worse, you will be alone.

Don't black me because you can't figure out or even digest what I am thinking, even when you sometimes pretend you know. Don't black me. I am made of hope, even when it seems I am swimming in an ocean of hopelessness, engulfed in all its predicaments and consequences.

Don't black me. Life has been rude to me. Still, it has brought me foundations based on hope. Don't black me. I am here. And if not for a purpose, why am I here? Do you know the truth about me? If so, why didn't I know that you knew?

I tried to look for the truth in the scriptures, but there you are—who wrote the scriptures? I tried to look for the truth in my environment, but there you are waiting.

I tried to search for the truth in my own religion. There you are, telling me it's not the right thing and that the truth you found is the one and only truth.

But do you really know the truth? I believed you, and you deserted me and even took away the promise my own religion and way of life had to offer.

Now I am naked, and all about me has been broken and scattered like the ashes of old. They say the sun is shining everywhere. However, there are those who have been denied the sunsets, not to mention its brightness.

Still, my hope is what has kept me here. I am here. I have been here. I will be here, even when you sometimes think I don't deserve to be. Can you change me? Can you really tell the birds where and when to fly? Can you tell the owl not to show itself at night? Are you seeing what the owl sees? Can you ask the moon not to give its light in the night and the sun not to shine in the day? Can you change the sun just like you change the electric bulbs? Can you ask the baby to change and give its first cry in the womb? Can you stop the graves from receiving? Can you even stop ears from receiving words, from being filled with them?

No. Don't black me, because this world is characterized by structures that may seem to limit our choices, which, in the end, may provide more opportunities.

I have life, and my hope is borderless and boundless. The world is full of life. Why are some finding it difficult to breathe? Why are some not even given the chance to breathe?

Don't "white" me, because I am engulfed in insecurities. Don't white me, because from the onset, I am left alone, go alone, and try alone. Don't white me. I am a lonely heart. I was not born with such hopes like you, and that's what I am trying to admit. I was born, and little did I learn to cry. I was thrown into that cart left to look for me, with me, by me, all by me. I never enjoyed the warmness of security like you.

I live with constant insecurities. That's what has shaped me, shaped my ways.

Like you, I have searched for the truth, but I have not been able to find it. So I decided to create what I will call truth, which I partly identify with, and I want you to believe it completely. But do I know the truth? I don't want to admit any insecurity in myself, so I keep pushing, seeking to defend and uphold my ground with all the necessary weapons known to humanity and me.

Do I feel sometimes that I know better than you do? Yes. But is this the reality in the common sense of life and its simplicity and complexity? Of course not.

I might be swimming in the physical glories of invention and conveniences, as far as life on earth is concerned, but inside, I am engulfed in insecurities and the constant search for new challenges. I am limited. This I know, but I don't want to admit this.

All the battles I've been involved in, has been about survival and challenges brought about by my tireless wanderings. I am a lonely man, and I know that life without you is not possible. But can I survive my insecurities? Are you not going to do to me what I did to you? Can we forgive each other? I know you don't trust me because of my actions and my insecurities, which you are not aware of and I am not willing to admit to. Now that I have the physical gains, what am I going to do with them? I want to see you as my able partner, in win-win games. But can I overcome my insecurities and fears? Let's stretch out those hands of trust to overcome our distrust and fears.

Let's be kind to one another. If we begin small, more shall join the light and leave darkness to darkness. In the end, we shall live like human beings and not other kinds of life on earth.

***

Paper German is about the everyday life of migrants and their children, the third and fourth generations who are living in Germany and Central Europe. It addresses not only the physical challenges but also the psychological challenges that foreigners face, in terms of equality, employment, education, and opportunities in life. It reveals the principles of denials that have long been engraved in the inner circle of a society known for its innovations and prosperity worldwide.

This psychological apartheid makes it almost impossible for people who are not ethnic Germans to realize their dreams in a country known for its peace initiatives and the promotion of human rights around the globe. The type of psychological denials that exist here in Germany are dealt out in small doses that might not be easily noticed by someone just passing. But the small doses add up and have a huge impact on the social, economical, and cultural heritage of migrants who call Germany their home.

I want to make this known because the truth needs to be told. I couldn't just leave things the way they are. It strikes me to my bones to know that if you are not born an ethnic German, you are only going to be engulfed in limitations—not because you are not willing or because you were born with certain limitations or had an accident that limits you, but because of your skin color; your ethnic background; your religion; and, above all, your identity. All these factors make it impossible to live one's own dream—of finding a decent, well-paying job, for example.

Many, like me, came to Germany soaring on puffy clouds of hope and brightness, only to find themselves swimming in the ocean of hopelessness, the shores growing more distant every time they attempt to swim. Even when they do manage to get to the shore, they are constantly reminded that their place is in the ocean of hopelessness and that they will never achieve their goals, so long as they are on German soil.

This is the condition that exists right here in Germany. These denials don't just limit older migrants. They affect their children too.

It all starts from an early age, when a child is around three years old and continues, virtually nonstop, until he or she is an adult. That's how migrants live. They seem to accept the situation because of the social systems meant to help for a while. These systems, though, do not last for life. Here, you have generations living from social benefits. The effect is that you have people who would have, in one way or the other, succeeded in a job and lived with dignity instead living from crumbs fallen from the master's table, like dogs waiting to be given food and commands, without the ability to make real decisions of their own.

This country has vast experience with suffering and wars coupled with racism and destruction. I want the lessons learned from all that chaos to be extended to modern days and to migrants. Migration is as old as humanity itself. If given equal opportunities, migrants can contribute to and benefit the societies in which they live—in most cases, the only society they have ever known. This book provides insight into the real society that I have lived in for twenty years and the one I now call home, even though, after all these years, I still don't feel as though I'm being taken seriously, be it socially, economically, culturally, or otherwise.

Having outlined these denials, I believe there is hope that, one day, my little children will be treated with the dignity they deserve—that their treatment will be based on equality and that everyone will have equal opportunities, regardless of their skin color or religion. After all, "Hoffnung stirbst zu letzt" (Hope dies last). I have life, and when there is life, there is hope. Hope is strong. Hope is endless, tireless, and timeless. But as a carrier of hope and dreams, I am endless, tireless, timeless. Well, read my stories.

1

My name is Peter Emwindearu Omoregbe, and I was born October 23, 1970, in the ancient city of Bini, which is in southwestern Nigeria, to Pa Vincent Ohuimumwen Omoregbe and Mrs. Felicia Imwenoghomwen Omoregbe at about eleven at night in a neighbor's house.

My mother is my dad's fifth wife, and I am her first child in my father's house. She lost her first man in the Biafran Civil War of the sixties. My dad delightedly took in her other three children and treated us all as his.

He never treated the other children badly and even sent them to school. I received beatings from my dad as a child, but he never touched the other children. In his words, "I never knew my dad, and they'll never know their dad either. So we share, in some ways, the same destiny. But for you, Peter, you are my son. You know me, and I want you to know me for real."

My God, living with him was, indeed, very tough. Every morning before going to school, I was to clean his chairs in the living room; his old refrigerator, which he'd bought shortly before my birth; and, later, in the eighties, his 504 saloon car.

My father was happy to have a son, and so he gave my mum all the best attention she deserved for three months. Thereafter, he left her to fend for herself, though he supported her sometimes. Once the three-month period of being on bed rest was over, the women were on their own.

When a woman had just been put on bed rest, she didn't have to wash the dishes, she got the best food, and the house was automatically filled with all kinds of foods not normally in the house.

My dad went even further, buying his wives Bournvita, a chocolate drink. He had heard that such drinks helped women who had just given birth to regain their strength and alleviated the stress brought on by babies during the night. Drinking Bournvita was even supposed to help new mothers produce more milk.

The relatives of my mother and those of my father were all there twenty-four hours a day, and all of them did their parts with utmost joy. These kinds of treatments are very rare these days. This kind of love, for example, when a woman has just given birth, is what I really miss as an adult.

***

I grew up with other kids in the ancient city of Benin, around four hundred kilometers from Lagos, the former capital of Nigeria.

My father was a plumber and a local real estate agent. My mum was a petty trader, who sold and bought foodstuffs in the suburban villages. I grew up with polygamy and all its experiences. I saw progress and developments. I saw and experienced failures as well. Some of the bitterness associated with polygamy still exists to this day.

My dad didn't know his dad and was raised by his grandfather. His mum later told me that his father died when he was four months old.

He wanted all his children to be educated. "Anyone who cannot read or write is a blind fellow," he would say. He said he once wept for three days after he was approached by an English supervisor in the fifties and asked to write his name. The supervisor said that if he could do so, he would be made the head of other workers and would receive all the benefits of such a position. The supervisor appreciated in my father a sense of responsibility and decency. But my dad couldn't write his name. Hence, he could not get the job. At that time, in the fifties, he worked as a plumber for the federal ministry of works and housing in Benin.

I could not because I was not given the chance to even try. And so, my father vowed that all his children would be educated. He even sponsored his firstborn's travel to Australia in the seventies to attend a university there.

While our older brother was away in Australia, he took sole responsibility for sending the remaining children to school in Nigeria. Sometimes, my mum said, it was very difficult to feed us kids because my dad had already spent the money on education, both home and abroad. At that time, we were around fifteen children, and at his death in 1997, we were twenty-five children.

***

I went to primary school with six. I remember my mum took me to the school building. I was so excited. I war my school uniform, which had been sewn by the father of my father's first wife (Ewemade). It was a great day for me. I really liked when the teacher came before us, greeted us, and prayed with us in our traditional language. I still remember the words of the prayer:

> Oh God, we are your little children—we and all the children of the world. Protect us all as we cross the streets. Protect us from sickness that would prevent us from coming to school. Help us to obey our parents and our elders so that we can dwell on earth for longer. Let wisdom and goodness of heart follow us all the days of our lives. Amen.

Then we would recite poems in which our teacher would say a line and we students would respond together. "Pussycat, pussycat, where have you been?" the teacher would begin.

"I have been to London to see the queen," we would reply.

We would all laugh and jump as high as we could.
I remember my father asking me, "Do you like going to school?"
"Yes," I told him.

He would laugh and dance with us kids, and he even shared with us chocolate called goodie goodie. It was the best chocolate I'd ever eaten. To this day, I still remember the taste of the chocolate, and I would recognize it should I ever get hold of some.

After my primary education, I proceeded to my secondary education in 1982. In the 1987/88 school year, I got my GCE ordinary level certificate.

2

In 1989, there was a great deal of unrest in Nigeria. Teachers were striking, jails were broken into—some the criminals who ran away were recaptured later, but many just went underground—and students were dissatisfied with the system. Hungry students were learning by candlelight, and lecturers bargained with students, offering good scores for sex. Those who were supposedly running the affairs of a nation didn't take on an iota of responsibility. Rather, in effect, they were there to steal, kill, maim, and disorganize and to create a chaotic environment so that the looting could go on unnoticed.

With all this confusion and uncertainty, I started looking for solutions. I found the answer I had been looking for in traveling overseas. My other brothers had left for Germany in 1988, and I was dreaming of moving out too. I told my mother about my plan. She was not so happy about the idea. I convinced her, pointing out that our neighbors' children were all away and assuring her that if I moved out, I would continue with my education.

Eventually, she promised to talk to my father about it, and because of the good relationship she shared with him, she was eventually able to convince him.

I had even asked her to take a closer look at the situation in Nigeria. "I can't even study in peace here," I pointed out.

More than twenty years later, the situation has gone from worse to worst. I recall that, in 1980, my father bought his first pickup delivery van for 4,000 naira and a brand-new Peugeot 504 saloon limousine car for 7,871 naira and 81 kobo. The receipts are still available. Today in Nigeria, you can't even get used (and almost worn out) tires for this amount. Perhaps, for 4,000 naira, you could get some used shoes from Europe.

Nigeria fell in love with used items—they call it *belgium* or *tokunbo*—not because they love used stuff but because it's the easiest way to survive.

***

Nigerians pray to God in desperation. There are already clergymen waiting to squeeze the very last drops out of them. These men give them false hopes and instill in them fear, convincing them that, if they don't pay their tithes, they might meet their sudden deaths.

An average Nigerian man spends most of his time in the church. You can find him there seven days of the week, and every second night you'll find a prayer warrior, speaking out against demons and witches. You'll hear unfounded claims, such as, "AIDS is the devil's work." The devil is held responsible for virtually every mishap that befalls people.

On an average Nigerian street, you'll find no less than ten churches, all built with planks and zincs. Some even look like kiosks for selling newspapers. Others are two-room buildings; the clergyman lives in one of the rooms, and the other is the church.

These clergymen always preach about evils and torments, the devil and the troubles of the world. They shout and speak in tongues. Some even attempt to raise the dead. Others coastal far as to prophesize that God spoke to them and that, therefore, they are anointed directly by God.

Who am I to judge these multiple liars acting on the frustrations of the common man, who has already been victimized by those in authority and in positions to help him? Those who could help tend to refrain from doing so because of selfish desires for gains, which only last for a while.

Some clergymen even use fear to seduce women and break up happy homes. It is not uncommon for married women to wash the clothes of the pastor's wife, their children, and the pastor himself. The argument is that, if they undertake this task, "the grace of God will automatically come to you."

By their introductions, these clergymen call themselves men of God.

There are some who are so strategic in this business of holiness that they can afford private jets fuelled and maintained by politicians. You see, these are all factors that every Nigerian you see on your streets or on planes has to deal with directly or indirectly.

Such corrupt practices are encouraged by those who claim to have moral authority. These so-called authorities are part of the cancer eating through the common man in Nigeria.

Married women and young girls are given mandates to lure customers to the banks, when necessary with sex, or risk being sacked by their bosses. People's fear of losing jobs makes them desperate. In the last breath of desperation, they tend to lose their grip on moral control. Thereby, thing fall apart, and it becomes impossible for people to hold onto their centers—what keeps them grounded.

3

I HAVEN'T EXPLAINED MY BACKGROUND. I will now focus on the reasons I decided to write *Paper German*.

I traveled to Germany twenty-two years ago. Upon my arrival, I was made to understand that the only way to work and stay in Germany was to get a residence permit (called *Aufenthaltsgenehmigung*). The quickest way to do that was to marry someone with German citizenship or get some kind of refugee status.

I eventually got to know Agathe, who I actually married, not so that I could stay but because of who she was to me at the time. We got along very well, but her parents, like many parents, were totally against interracial marriage. The scars of that rejection still exist to this day.

After our marriage in 1994, I started looking for employment. Eventually, I landed a job with a furniture company. In the meantime, I also visited a language school.

The language school lasted three months, and I could now read and write German. Though my German wasn't perfect, I now started exploring my environment and planning my future. Meanwhile, Agathe was unhappy with my future plans. She wanted me to have a job that was secure, even if that meant cleaning toilets or working in a warehouse. It didn't matter what my work was, provided it was guaranteed to last for a long time. I had my reservations, though.

That gave me the courage to go on to attend the German school of economics. I obtained a certificate for wholesale and international trade. Agathe remained concerned. It wasn't that she didn't want me to have a profession, but she was afraid that, after my graduation and all the effort I had put toward obtaining my certificate, I would still be relegated to cleaning and services jobs, a common situation. These types of jobs were almost the only accessible options for foreigners and migrants, and that was true even for the second and third generations of immigrants.

They say it takes a village to raise a child, but I would say a child can also raise a town, cities, and even a country. For example, JP Morgan bailed the United States government out of bankruptcy many years ago; that was a single person helping to rescue a country from falling.

Mr. Morgan was able to carry out such a rescue missions because he had the opportunity, and the environment he lived him enabled him, giving him access to the resources he needed to take on such an undertaking. We are all dependent on a child's developments in our everyday activities, either directly or indirectly, from the moment we stand up in the mornings to the time we retire to bed in the evenings. We are dependent on others throughout our lives and even in our deaths, as a vehicle must convey our corpses to the cemetery.

Vehicles were invented many years ago by an adult who was once a child. We all enjoy the benefits and convenience vehicles afford us today, and so will the generations that come after us.

Now we might want to ask ourselves, what does the migrant situation in Germany have to do with JP Morgan bailing out the United States? It is obvious that Mr. Morgan had what I will call an enabling, encouraging environment. He lived in a Society where people saw the potential in anything moving, except the dead.

A person can only unlock his or her maximum potential if he or she is encouraged, included, enabled, and given a sense of belonging to the society they live.

Now, in the German society, as a foreigner, you are constantly reminded of your background, and you are always, knowingly or unknowingly, marginalized. This is the case when it comes to employment, and it's equally true in both the political and social arenas.

All of these problems start at an early age, often when children are as young as three years old. For example, consider the TV stations for children. You hardly see children with migrant background playing with the ethnic German children. Every example of what a person can be or achieve is given in the form of an ethnic German.

This carries on into a person's adult years and lasts until he or she has reached the pension age.

I recall a children's written for toddlers. A picture and it depicts a group of Indians sitting on the back of an elephant. Written on the side of the elephant is the word *taxi*. The same book includes a picture of a black child sitting with monkeys and a banana in between them. To me, books like these don't encourage children to be inclusive. They are likely to give, weather indirectly or not, young ethnic German children the impression that they are better than or have higher standards than others.

Under normal circumstance, integration for immigrants means the ability to interact in the local language and the willingness to respect the mentality of the local culture. Then people are allowed to settle in and focus on the purpose that brought them to their new home in the first place. In the case of migrants or foreigners in Germany, you can integrate yourself all you want, you can respect the local culture as much as you possibly can, and you will still be only one thing—a foreigner (*Ausländer*). The stigma is right at the surface, even when no one talks about it. You can see it in people's body languages in stores, in your interactions with colleagues, and even with your own wife or husband.

Sometimes I ask myself, is this a built-in phenomenon? Is this mentality unique to this country? What makes a society be closed to foreigners?

Then it occurs to me that we are all human beings. We tend to think we are superior when someone wants something from us, especially when that person doesn't look like us or speak like us or move like us. We even blame "outsiders" sometimes for our own frustrations with life or general discontent with the society. For example, after the fall of the Berlin Wall, Germans from the eastern part of the country came out with the slogan, "Ausländer raus Deutschland für Deutsche" (Foreigners get out; Germany for the Germans).

In fact there are some places in the eastern part of the country where people like me could be chased on the streets like chicken and rounded up like goats. This was not an uncommon scene in the nineties. Even these days, asylum seekers' hostels are burnt to rubble; black people are killed because of their skin color; and the slogan, "Ausländer nehmen unser arbeit weg" (Foreigners are taking away our jobs), is rampant.

In truth, in the areas where this attitude is prevalent, migrants make up only 1 percent of the total population. The slogan does not correspond to any known elements of truth. In truth, if an employer needs to fill a job vacancy and asks his or her secretary to select the best ten applicants, 9.5 of those selected will be ethnic Germans.

This is partly why it is rare for immigrants or foreigners to hold white-collar positions or public office. The same is true for both the police force and the army. Neither do immigrants hold positions in prison management. I have never, in my twenty years in Germany, seen a black man going to the office wearing a necktie.

In addition to this marginalization, children with migrant backgrounds aren't encouraged in schools in the same way their ethnic German counterparts are.

There are two major sectors in which you can find a large proportion of foreigners—the service industry (holding jobs like cleaning) and the warehouses. And even at these "mediocre" jobs, supervisory posts are always occupied by Germans.

***

Two years ago, I went to a seminar to learn about paramedic and rescue techniques. We participants, about eight of us, were asked to introduce ourselves. I introduced myself as a Nigerian, though I have German nationality. I chose to introduce myself this way because I knew what questions would follow if I were to make the mistake of introducing myself as a German: Were you adopted? Were you born here? Why do you speak accent-free German? Um, you've stayed in Germany for such a long time.

A similar thing happens when I tell people my name is Peter. There is always this frown on their faces. Sometimes, they cannot contain themselves, and they say what they're thinking outright. "Aber das ist aber Deutsche name" (That is just a German name).

One of the participants was a girl about twenty-two years of age. She was about to commence her studies at the university. She said she was from Heidelberg.

The teacher looked at her, not knowing what to say to her. Finally, he said, "Aber du bist kein biodeutsche" (You are not a biological German).

At first, there was silence in the room. Some of the participants laughed. Some frowned. But the message was clear—you are lying.

The problem with this girl was with her color. Her mum was Indian, and her father was German.

This wasn't the first time I'd heard this kind of psychological insult. On another occasion, I was in a class to learn how to drive a forklift. Once again, we had to introduce ourselves, sharing where we came from, what we intended to become, and so on. One student said he was German, and this teacher, like the other one, questioned him. "Did I just hear you say you're German?" The teacher asked.

The man in question said that he was, and he brought out his identity card and international passport.

The teacher replied, "Das ist nur papier auch schäferhund sind auch deutsche" (A passport is only paper. Even German schäferdogs are German).

Guess what? This guy was sad for the entire day.

***

While these views don't represent the views of the entire German society or all German people, they are shared by a lot of people, some of whom are very open and candid about their feelings. The primary reason for the economic and technological success of Germany is that the country is good at systematic organization. Such a system does not necessarily change but has the potential of revolving endlessly around its own axis. It also has the potential also for a sudden fall, as everything must change.

Many migrants went to Germany (and emigrants to countries around the globe) in search of meanings to life, employment, and better lives. However you look at it, people leave their natural habitats in search of greener pastures and, in the case of people coming from war-torn countries, security.

The movement of people (exodus) has been happening since humankind first came into existence. People have moved to tend livestock and for many other reasons.

Once migrants arrive in Germany, in most cases, they tend to seek asylum or the rare job opportunity. Asylum seekers are given the basic necessities of life, such as shelter, clothing, and food. These are all good things to start with, but in life, one is expected to move on. This is human, not criminal. If you want to move forward as a foreigner in Germany, that's where the long battles start. A newcomer to Germany is expected to maintain the same life he or she started with there—doing the mediocre jobs; living off social welfare; being pushed around like balls; and living in his or her own shadows, concerned primarily about paying the bills year in year out, without any focus.

It is not that the way to education is blocked. The question is whether you will be taken seriously after you get the right qualifications or even the right profession. Many, if not all, white-collar jobs are reserved for Ethnic Germans (*biodeutsche*). It is not uncommon to see pensioners still hanging around offices and giving instructions, while there are many qualified young people seeking to be employed. In many cases, the old pensioner is waiting to leave the job until someone he or she knows to apply for the position; this is referred to as *Vitamin B Beziehung*. It's how unqualified people sometimes find their ways into top jobs, leaving others to wonder how this happened.

Many migrants were educated in their various home countries but end up cleaning offices because they figure, why try? After all, I'm not going to end up being able to use what I have to achieve better results.

For example, in my own case, my GCE ordinary level certificate in Nigeria was only seen as *Hauptschulabschluss* (a primary school leaving certificate).

Agathe, my wife at the time, once told me, "You go to work and go to evening classes as well. Why are you committing yourself to something that is not going to bring you any good? You can be educated as much as you can but no one is going to employ you for this, even if you are qualified."

She pointed out that many foreigners knew this to be true; this was why they decided to be cleaners, kitchen helpers, or construction helpers. "And you—you want to be something else," she said, her tone and accusatory, as if moving on was a crime.

Now, if someone who lived with me could be so negative about the prospect of a foreigner getting a good and well-paid job, then you can imagine what someone who had nothing to do with me might think or say. I don't hold any grudges against Agathe because her views are a product of the society we live in.

Meanwhile, I enrolled in evening classes to get my high school degree (*mittlerereife*). After two years of evening classes, I finally had my degree.

4

I DON'T KNOW WHO IS reading this book. Regardless of who you are, what your position is, or the color of your skin, I want you to believe in one thing—follow your heart in all you do, think, or say. I am thoroughly convinced that we are own best oracles.

And there is no one who is not productive. We are all special in different ways and adept at different thing. We all have one thing in common, and that's the desire to be loved. No one wants to be marginalized in any aspect of life. It hurts.

***

After the successful completion of my high school degree, I decided to learn a profession. I settled on salesmanship and international trade and asked my boss if I could do the practicals at the company whose warehouse I had worked in for nearly seven years. In Germany, learning a profession requires a combined parallel theory and practicals program of study. You get the theory at the school and then do the practicals with a company. This is mandatory for all those who want to learn a profession. Depending on the student's education level and experience, the program takes two to three years to complete.

My boss agreed to my request, and a contract was signed to this effect. For the next two years, I saw myself running between school and the company. At the school, a lot of fun was to be had. I was enrolled alongside students who could well be my children. The other students and I got along very well. I was even made the class spokesperson.

The company, however, was a different thing altogether. In fact, if I had been a little bit younger, I would have given up on my studies. We must learn to engage people without discouraging them. After all, who knows? What you do to me I might do to you.

The envy I experienced from the people I worked with at the company was greater than anything I could have imagined. It was obvious that I was going to be confronted with a degree of envy. But I hadn't imagined it could strike me right in the center of my heart and soul.

Here was a guy who used to wear warehouse clothes, and now he was wearing an office uniform, sometimes even a necktie, and making conversations with customers. Many people took this personally.

Those in charge of teaching me the practicals totally ignored me. Every day, I was instructed only to clean the coffee machine, take letters to the post office, and collect the garbage from the dustbins. On occasion, I was told to look through the list of the company's debtors.

The psychological torture had soon taken its toll on me. Still, I was determined to go through with what I had started and finish the job of becoming a salesman (*Kaufmann*).

Sometimes we are not responsible for our troubles and struggles and even whether or not we have ambitions. We do, however, have the ability to make choices; choice making is our responsibility.

Why must a man's dream be rendered invalid by his fellowman simply because of his skin color, gender, ethnicity, race, or other identifying characteristics? The world has never been a better place than it is in the twenty-first century. That we are all connected—whether we live in towns, villages, or cities—and the way that is beginning to even out the playing field in terms of opportunity is a blessing in its own right.

But why are there so many troubles and so many wars? Why is there so much suffering? Why are beautiful cultural heritage sites being destroyed? Why are we not enjoying the beauty life today has to offer? Why are we not satisfied with our lives? Why do we feel lonely in spite of all the fun gadgets out there? Where did we get it wrong?

The envy and bitterness went on and on, but I was determined to complete the course.

I believe that we are our own best teachers. I know you might want to say, that's easier said than done. There is no way to ever completely satisfy human beings. The only time we can be satisfied is when we are lying in our caskets. So be determined to let your heart lead you, irrespective of friends, relatives, or anyone else.

Those tasked with heading my program at the company were reluctant to teach me the necessary skills I needed for my profession. I even heard one of them say, "Our boss says yes to anything." They were calling him a *Jasager* (yes-man). I was like a pest or, better yet, a burden.

Moreover, I did not fit into many people's picture of immigrants or foreigners. They expected "us" to be living at the mercy of social welfare and unemployment benefits or doing unskilled, low-paid labor. The same people who used to laugh and crack jokes with me during my years in the warehouse were now behaving as if I was an alien. Their mockery was clear in their body language and in the smiles across their faces.

The boss at the time was not helpful. This was never more pronounced then when he said to me, upon my graduation, "Deutschland ist was es ist, ich glaube nicht das jemand dich jemals einstellen wird als kaufmann du bist kein Weiss" (Germany is what it is. I don't believe anyone will ever employ you as salesman. You are not white.).

I was shocked. Well, his proclamation did not represent my own version of my ability, so I just thought to myself, *You are not God.* I was convined within my heart of hearts that I was going to get myself what I was worth.

Get yourself what you are worth. Don't be discouraged by the circumstances around you. Even when it seems there is no way out, the chance for you to exhale will come. What we pray for is the recognition of that defining moment in our lives.

***

In order to complete the salesmanship profession program, one is expected to have all practical knowledge of the various sections in a company—from the warehouse to the accounting and transport logistics departments and all the various departments in between. As I continued my pursuit of a career, the situation remained nearly the same. I still wasn't taken seriously, and it was the direct result of envy and the psychological isolation of those who do not look like the majority.

When you are confronted with this kind of psychological alienation, all you need do is examine the reasons why you are there in the first place. Take it head on. Remember that it has nothing to do with you. It has something to do with those who are finding it difficult to live with others. Keep moving forward and have a "plan B" ready, because, if one fails to plan, one may be planning to fail.

I moved to the accounting department. A particular woman in the department took every step I made very personally. One morning, she could no longer resist. "Du sollst wissen was hier los ist," she said to me. This statement, on the surface, simply means, "You should know what is happening here." Someone who understands the German mentality and cultural realizes it's real meaning is, "You are not welcome here in any form." She shouted as loudly as she could.

I simply replied, "Ich bin nicht hier für dich" (I am not here for you).

She was then silent, but somehow I was disappointed that her boss, who was in the next office, did not do anything to rebuke or caution her.

***

The kind of "look on" attitude display by that boss in the accounting office is very common in Germany. However, I am impressed to find that, these days, many people are summoning the courage to confront those who demonstrate against foreigners, protesting against *überfremdung* (foreign infiltration).

Now in the news media, one keeps hearing phrases like, "We need more civil courage." In reality, though, phrases like these are meant to portray a good image and buy time.

There are some areas, especially in the eastern part of the country, where your physical appearance and the color of your skin could lead to beatings and even deaths.

There was the case of a schoolteacher who painted over a neo-Nazi symbol—a swastika (*Hakenkreuz*)—in a school building and was fined a thousand pounds for his actions. This was in 2014.

And there are many instances in which the life of a migrant is like grass in the fields you can use as feed for animals or simply burn to make space.

An African immigrant was brutally but systematically killed in the presence of police officers in 2005. Two policemen say they saw the man ingest something they suspected to be cocaine. He was arrested, and both his hands and legs were chained. A doctor was called in to make sure he vomited the substance he'd swallowed. A seventy-centimeter-long plastic tube was driven through his nose and into his stomach, and for the next two and a half hours, water and vomit-inducing substances were passed into his stomach. At this point, the man fell into a coma and died, apparently because water had gone into his lungs and he was drowned.

The doctor involved was charged twice but was also cleared twice. Only after heavy protesting was he made to pay twenty thousand pounds, and the whole case was forgotten.

There are many instances of beatings and racial prejudice against migrants by right-wingers and the people are never charged.

***

An advertisement on a placard carried the slogan, "Mehr toleranz für Ausländer" (More tolerance for foreigners). Well I say you don't tolerate people; you accept them.

It is only when you accept people with open arms that you give them the opportunity to unlock their potential and be active in the development of the society.

The roots of the United States of America's dominance of the world today do not lie in her military might or her economic success. Nor is that dominance a result of the purchasing power of her people. Rather, America's success is her ability to absorb and accept people the way they are—to see the positive in human beings and unlock that potential for the benefit of the society and the world at large.

There is no known ethnic group of the human race that doesn't have a millionaire representative in the United States because the principle there is that, if you work hard, you will be rewarded. Obviously this means that people will work hard—knowing that they will, at last, be rewarded.

I went to the United States last July. While there, I attended a graduation ceremony for a group of kindergarten children in Lynn, Massachusetts. I met a Sudanese child who said to the audience that he would like to become a police officer. He spoke with full confidence written across his face. I was perplexed, and at the same time, I loved the confident nature of this seven-year-old. I saw the society he lives in speaking through him.

I went to visit the North Shore Community College in Lynn. The welcoming nature of the people there was awesome. The people I met at the college advised me on how to study, informed of what I needed, and even told me I could book a session with a counselor who would offer more advice. I saw this opportunity and asked myself, *Am I on another planet or here on earth?*

Now I am not saying America does not have its own dark sides, but the notion of equal opportunity actually works there.

As an immigrant in Germany, whether or not you possess German nationality, your dreams are limited. For example, if that Sudanese child were living in Germany, he wouldn't even be able to join the police force; no one would accept him. A mixed race child once told his mum of his intention to join the police force. His mum, who happens to be white, immediately told him he had better not make that mistake because, as she said, "You will suffer the worst humiliations of your life." She went on to tell him that, even if he were accepted, he wouldn't be thought of as having the "right stuff." She concluded, "You will suffer mobbing to the highest order."

Another immigrant said he would like to be a banker. But before you can learn anything about banking, you must find a bank that accepts you for practicals. Not one bank would take the man on because of his origin. These are all children who were born and bred in this country, and yet they are alienated in their own country.

This kind of marginalization of humans can lead to situations of havoc, which, with simple methods could be averted. Simply put, we must give all people—regardless of their race or color—the opportunity to discover and live their dreams.

***

The Turkish people first came to this country more than fifty years ago, and they form the largest ethnic minority group here in Germany. Yet they are underrepresented in all aspect of human endeavor in the German society. They have the highest number of dropouts from schools, and society seems to be tying every setback to their fate imaginable. Some even argued they are not willing to be integrated.

No human being with an appropriate sense of humanity doesn't want to be treated with dignity and respect. The fact is Turkish people in Germany are being pushed around, directly or indirectly, by the only society they know. They are marginalized by the society they seem to represent but are not a part of.

Most Turkish citizens are frustrated with the society they live in, as opportunities are rare. Most end up setting up kebab shops or grocery and vegetables shops or selling used vehicles and living from social benefits. A few exceptions can be found—Turkish lawyers and doctors and other professionals. These are rare, though, perhaps one in twenty.

5

AFTER MY GRADUATION FROM THE school of sales and international trade, I was asked to go back and work in the warehouse of the same company where I had completed my practicals. I rejected this offer and have no regrets about turning it down, even though it marks the beginning of my long struggle to find decent employment— something other than the ever-available unskilled, low-wage jobs.

In life, we all deserve to be paid what we are worth, and you should not settle for anything less, no matter who you are or what you do. So long as you've been able to prove yourself and you love what you are doing, you deserve the rightful incentives. It's your birthright and a right of life.

Eventually, I started my own business, selling hospital furniture to Nigeria, my native country. The business was quite lucrative at first. But problems with the business environment, including corruption at the seaports, make it difficult for importers to break even. This, coupled with lawlessness in the country, compelled me to withdraw from this business.

The experience, however, exposed me to some realities of life— realities related to the common man in a country with a wealth of natural resources that is yet unable to provide hospital beds for its citizens. We have able doctors in Nigeria, lots of them, but they are not equipped with the right tools. Some instruments being used by health care professionals date back to the seventies. Still, yet the doctors in Nigeria are able to perform their duties. They need the kind of support I have been talking about in this book from the government—which tends to run the country as if it is private property, thereby endangering the lives of millions of Nigeria's citizens.

As a result, the people of Nigeria are scattered around the globe like sheep without shepherds, living in constant fear in their various countries of choice. Young boys and girls take great risk to travel on high seas, loaded like chickens into shipping compartments, only to be dumped in barricaded confinements that amount to prison yards. The cry for help is not being heard by those who are supposed to be listening.

These young people were sent on a journey of exile without return tickets by their own government, which cares only for its own needs. The Nigerian government cares more about looting the treasury than it does for its citizens. Billions of stolen money is stockpiled around the globe, with the best securities imaginable.

Nigerians are coming to Europe in the hundreds and thousands, at great risk, in search of a better life, which may never materialize. Even when they eventually make it to mainland Europe, they are made to understand that they can only be tolerated (*duldung*) and can never be accepted in their new society. Many of these refugees turn to prostitution or drugs and, often, land in jail as a result.

***

Recently, there was a debate on how to tackle the lack of professional workers in different sectors of the economy. One aspect of the debate considered making it easier for people with professional experience to come from other countries and work here in Germany. A suggestion was that these professionals be given green cards, or blue cards as some wanted to call them, following similar models in Canada, the United States, and Australia.

Such changes are all easier said than done. Making immigration laws in Germany similar to those in Canada or the United States won't work. Here's why. The cultural differences between these countries are enormous. Similar ideas were attempted at the beginning of 2000 and 2002, when Germany requested that twenty thousand computer programmers come from India and Indonesia. Heavy debates among politicians ensued.

Some politicians even took the debate personally, saying things like, "Kinder staat indersoll an computer" (children should go to computer instead of Indians). Another statement Heard round the debate table was, "Elephanten verkäufer hat keine ahnung von computer" (Elephant sellers have no ideas about computer).

Of the twenty thousand requested computer expatriates, only ten thousand came, and of the ten thousand, only seven thousand actually stayed. Of those seven thousand, maybe a handful are still in Germany today.

Immigrants to Germany (and those seen as foreign, whether born in Germany or not) will not find in this country an environment that enables them to succeed. Rather, they will be considered suspect. It isn't that people will think you are a thief or a criminal. Rather, because you look foreign, they will find everything about you strange. You can see this almost immediately, from the body language of people you engage with and from their conversations with you. You are automatically on the receiving end. But how can you tell how many rooms are in a house without entering the house? This suspicious mentality makes it very difficult for many Germans to accept others, and that's where the problems lies.

***

Having said that, I believe there is hope. After all, if one does not change, the change will definitely come on its own, and the price one pays for the change that comes on its own is often bigger than what one would have paid if one had made the change by oneself.

I know it is the nature of humans to protect and preserve what they have, who they are, and where they live. However, there is also the danger of things falling apart when we do not accept that we don't have power over things that were meant to be, no matter how we try. Migration has no limit—no matter how you try to stop it or control it. It as old as humankind itself. Migration is as perfect as nature. Try to stop the birds from migrating from one place to the other, or ask the graves to stop receiving customers. So it is with migration. No one can stop migration.

I believe that the lack of expatriates in Germany can be linked to lack of acceptance and a reluctant, aging society that doesn't recognize the need to incorporate and integrate migrants into the society. If you are looking for a warehouse attendant, for example, you are going to surrounded with applicants. If you are looking for an engineer, a computer programmer, a kindergarten tutor, or teachers in schools, on the other hand, you are going to have a hard time finding someone. The reasons for this situation are obvious. The system doesn't encourage migrants to take or study for professional jobs. The society is aging. In addition to these social problems, there are also economic issues as far as pay is concerned.

An engineer, for example, receives less pay in Germany than he or she would in the United States, Canada, or the United Kingdom. Therefore, students at the university are finishing their studies and migrating elsewhere. This happens year in and year out. The vacuum left behind cannot be filled by those who remain, a large proportion of whom are not professionals. Again, because of the noninclusive nature of the society, qualified migrants would only see Germany as an alternative to nothing, even if they do not want to admit this.

I know of people who were pushed around in Germany without jobs, living on social benefits even when they had studied hard. When they made the decision to try their abilities somewhere else, they became successful in their newfound land.

Due to lack of opportunities for migrants, many have found a safe haven in cleaning jobs or kitchen jobs or as helpers of different kinds, be it in the construction sector or the driving sector. These are all jobs that don't require special education or skills and, as such, offer low pay. With these kinds of wages, the future is not bright. You will always be living "month to month," finding that your salary can only sustain you until the next paycheck comes. Or you might find yourself living on overdraft. Now tell me, how can one ever plan for the future with this kind low-paying job?

It is no secret that, if you have not inherited assets from your parents, relatives, friends, or some other benefactor or you don't have employment that pays well, the dream of owing a house is actually going to remain forever a dream. Some do build their own houses, but those houses are actually and completely paid for by the family's second and third generations.

A lot of migrants have given up on their dreams due to frustrations. They have come to believe that, even if they try, they will, in the end, be grouped as "outsiders." As a result, nothing actually changes. Many of them resort to the services jobs and then get a little help from the state. That's how we live—living lives very close to our shadows. Yet our destinations and dreams are far from our shadows because the society we want to belong to indirectly denies us the keys to living fulfilling lives.

Other migrants resort to self-employed businesses. This is especially prevalent in the transportation and courier sector, where one can drive on a personal account for large companies. This is referred to as *selbständige unternehmer*. Many migrants work in this sector. This type of self-employments entails you owning the delivery vans yourself. You are responsible for maintenance and repair of the van, and you are delivering for the company, for example the Deutsche Post. You will get a contract from the company, and then you will be authorized to collect and deliver letters in the company's name.

You are then given a fixed price for your work, say four thousand euros a month. Now for many migrants, this seems like a large sum of money. Here are the difficulties with this type of contract.

Consider your fixed costs, which include repaying the purchase of the van, which was likely bought on credit; the maintenance and repair costs associated with keeping the van on the road; and the cost of gas and other bills that must be paid, in addition to your health insurance, which you have to pay on your own. After taking care of all these costs, you are probably going to be left with nine hundred euros. You have a family to take care of and/or rent to pay. Before you know it, the money is gone. Many of these self-employed contractors end up living on overdrafts.

I once worked by the Deutsche Post. One day, I asked my boss if I could get a contract to become a self-employed worker for the Deutsche Post. He simply said, "Du bist bei uns als direkt arbeiter auf die sichere seite all diese selbständgen sind in große schulden manche kann ohne überziehungen bei der jeweilige banken nicht überleben" (You are on the safer side with as a direct employee. These self-employed people are in great debt. Some of them cannot survive without overdrafts from their various banks). After that, I observed that all the people who participated in this self-employed business with the post were foreigners—Russians, Turks, and Africans.

These are all desperate attempts by migrants to survive in a society that does not receive them well.

Three out of four migrants in Germany have no profession. Even whose who do are not going to be employed because of discrimination in the labor markets. A large proportion of foreigners are living off of social and unemployment benefits. The delicate thing about this is that, among some ethnic groups, many families have now been living in this situation generation after generation right here in Germany.

These human inequalities, if left unchecked, will have vast negative effects, not only on the German society, but also on Europe as a whole, as Germany is the engine on which Europe revolves. There will also be the effect of too many migrant youth growing up to be "clothed beggars," most of whom would have done far better had they met with open-armed integration into the German society.

The kind of societal inequalities that exist in Germany may not be physical, like those that existed in the United States in the sixties. What happens in Germany is a psychological alienation of foreigners, engraved in a system that makes it almost impossible for non-Germans to move forward in life and to live their dreams.

Germany is not an immigrant land in the sense that is a place where newcomers can live out their dreams. It is an immigrant land in terms of masses pouring in, especially from Eastern Europe, to take advantage of the welfare systems. But life is not just about living on welfare. Life is about fulfilling one's own dreams.

It took me twenty years to fully understand this psychological alienation of foreigners, and its effects are like a ticking bomb.

A few years ago, corruption charges related to party finances were brought against a state governor in Hessen. A debate on how to proceed with the allegations broke out in the state house floor. A member of the opposition party, who happened to be one of the few tolerated immigrants in such a position, was trying to challenge the character of the governor in question. He was still speaking when a member of the governor's party shouted, "Gehen sie zurück nach Sanai" (Go back to Sanai). He said this because the opposition member happened to have a father who was originally from Yemen.

Now imagine yourself in the position of this opposition member, who was born in Germany to a German mother. How would you feel? We are all humans, and we all have something that could make us very sad and frustrated with life. The only thing that's really important in life is to be inclusive, because you want to be included.

THE RISE OF EXTREMISM TODAY could be traced to the fact that people are fed up with life. Even when they were born in a particular society they feel like they are treated differently, either directly or indirectly, which makes them feel worthless.

Once a person feels unworthy because of outside factors, he or she will do anything to please anyone who gives him or her the feeling of being worth something. He or she will even be ready to die while being giving praises and confirmed worthy.

The low rate of recruitments of US citizen to "death preachers gang" isn't just a result of the United States having good intelligence to intercept such recruitments. It is also related to the country's policy of accommodating and absorbing anyone who is willing to make a life for him or herself. The United States has a system in place. New arrivals are given an upper hand to succeed. Those who work with immigrants there aren't just showing you the way; they're accompanying you until you get there. There is no other place on the planet where the fruits of these policies are as evident as in the United States.

The democratic nature of the Unites States can never be exported directly as it exists there to other countries. The country's founding fathers came to Jamestown with dreams. They actually made their dreams come true. That success may have come at a price, but they lived their dreams, and their children are continuing that dream. Dreaming is a phenomenon that goes beyond human imagination and is borderless. Anyone who believes that dreams comes true will always have an edge, and that's what the United States of America is about.

I believe American democracy should be split so that different branches can meet the needs of regional democracy around the world. Diplomats should travel to promote the US brand of democracy on a face-to-face basis. That would be fatal to the world's security threats. Here's why. To some, because democracy is attached to freedom, it is a security threat—a threat to their personal interests. Hence, they would do anything to sabotage or completely eradicate it. In some people's beliefs, only those at the top should enjoy freedoms, and the masses should remain in captivity and darkness. This is the system that ensures their activities run smoothly. It is a complex world.

The German politician with a Yemeni background was being shouted at by his fellow lawmaker because the latter doesn't believe the former is entitled to criticize a full-blooded German (*biodeutsche*), as it was called by the teacher in the paramedic school. He doesn't believe that a man with a Yemeni background can ever be taken seriously. This belief, part of a system that doesn't view immigrants as equal partners, is widely spread throughout the country.

***

In 2009, someone broke into the apartment I shared with my girlfriend. We called the police, and some officers came to evaluate the situation. My girlfriend was present, along with her daughter and son from a previous relationship. We were all standing. The first thing one of the policemen did was to ask for my passport. No one else in the room was asked to show his or her identity documents.

This is another tactic to remind anyone that doesn't look like an ethnic Germans that he or she does not belong to the society and, as such, cannot be counted as equal.

If, for example, a conflict that warrants the presence of the police—even something as minor as traffic accident—involves a foreigner and two Germans, when the police arrive at the scene, the first thing they will do is ask the foreigner for his *Ausweis* (identity card). Only after that has been accomplished will they concentrate on the two Germans, asking for their versions of the incident. When the foreigner tries to give his or her own version of what happened, he or she will be ignored or asked to be quiet. In fact, from the very beginning of their arrival, the police officers will try to form a bond with the other two Germans while proceeding with their investigations, and the foreigner will be completely ignored.

***

Some children's book do, in fact, encourage racial prejudice or racial bias against immigrants, especially those with black or dark skin. One book, for example, features the "ten *neger*" (negroes). The book starts out with ten neger. A bird comes and eats one, and now nine neger remain. A snake comes and eats one of them. Now there are only eight. This goes on and on until no neger are left. Let's be frank with ourselves and say the truth. Is this the kind of book anyone should buy for his or her child? We all live in a world that is bound together with one force. Everything can be traced to one particular source. The only thing a river knows is to flow into the sea, and the price we pay for living is death.

By handing out this kind of book to children, you are indirectly telling them to see black people as enemies, who must not be seen around at all. You are indirectly creating within them hatred and racial bias toward people who do not look like them. Once such beliefs are engraved within a child's natural constitution, it becomes part of his or her behavior and views on matters and situations he or she faces in life.

So many people today are confused with their lives, and this is true even among those who are very successful. Daily, these people are confused and sad. Sometimes, they are aggressive—so much so that they do things like run into crowds and start shooting human beings—others who are human like themselves.

Where does all this hatred came from? Why are people so confused and sad, in spite of economic and social success? Why are there no known cures to so many psychological problems?

The lists of questions and problems are endless. The root cause of all of these problems, however, is clear. It can be found in lies and the creation of an atmosphere of fear in order to control, regulate, and have dominion over humankind. The perpetrators of these lies have a sole intention—to ride on the horse of power so that they can manipulate humanity and ensure they end up in the "jail of hell".

For nonethnic Germans and foreigners, psychological and institutional racism starts when they are as young as three years old. Sometimes, the kindergarten tutors are unaware of the damages they are doing to children by making them feel secluded. When a German child is having difficulties with the lessons, he or she is given the utmost attention. The teacher works with the child until he or she understands the lesson or makes progress.

But when a migrant child faces the same situation, struggling to understand the lessons, he or she is not encouraged. When this child pushes for answers, he or she is shunned or asked to be quiet—at threat of being stamped "hyperactive" or labeled with the pronouncement, "Diese kind ist durch den wind" (This child is uncontrollable).

If this does happen, the teacher will recommend that the parents seek the advice of a psychiatrist. And it doesn't end there. This child becomes everybody's "darling," in terms of giving them something to talk about—someone about whom to hand out judgments. All of this is, of course, to the detriment of this child, who was only seeking to understand the lessons being taught.

This string of events will have a domino effect on this child's life. He or she will become isolated from the mainstream lectures.

All in all, situation is going to make it difficult for the child to live his or her dreams.

A line of complaint heard at German schools attended by migrants is "Die sind doch Ausländische kinder" (These are all foreigners children.). Such complaint is followed by accusations such as, "They do not speak German with their children at home, and this is why the children do not understand the lessons."

These accusations may or may not be true. The families may or may not speak German language at home. Nevertheless, the root cause of the children's difficulty with the lessons still remains the unencouraging attitude at the school.

Now as to why these foreigners might be having problems with the German language, many understand that, whether or not they speak German, the end results will be the same. *No one will take me seriously*, they conclude, *so why should I bother?* Perfect German is not required to clean toilets.

***

The German school system is divided into three categories— *hauptschule* (middle school), *realschule* (secondary school), and *abitur* (high school or college). Anybody with good abitur grades can go on to study at the universities or polytechnics. The realschule is primarily for children who are better than those bound for hauptschule but whose performance falls short of abitur. Children who attend the realschule can still go in for abitur but must attend an extra year in the school. The hauptschule is for the children who need more attention and time to assimilate the lessons. If these students are lucky enough, they can get a workshop to learn a profession. The majority of migrant children are in the middle or secondary school categories.

Not long ago, the teachers were the ones who determined which of the categories a child fit into, in addition to the child's ability or academic performances.

A Turkish father changed the course of his son's life after the boy was recommended for the realschule. The father was determined that his child was far more capable than the teacher's recommendations suggested, so he enrolled his child in extra lectures. A year later, the child got his abitur. He now studies architecture at a university.

While the teacher's recommendation might not have been directly linked to the child's migrant status, loopholes in the system do not encourage diversity in terms of education and employment opportunities. This is very evident when you look at the makeup of staff in offices and at large organizations or among those who are in positions of authority across the board.

If that Turkish man had not taken such bold steps to encourage his son, perhaps the boy would have ended up attending realschule. That would have meant looking for a workshop where he could learn a trade, perhaps carpentry or plumbing. Or he might have studied to become a barber.

The next hurdle the young man will face is finding an employer to take him on for the practical aspect of his studies. Most companies would rather hire ethnic Germans over Turkish, black people, or anyone with a migrant background. If he is unable to find a place to complete the practicals, he might just end up having to be a shopkeeper in his uncle's kebab shop. Perhaps he will try and raise capital through his family and then secure a kebab shop of his own. Or he may end up selling used cars to Egypt or Nigeria or the Middle East.

While the above professions are not bad professions, they are saturated and, hence, not sustainable. There is no certainty in them, which means living in constant fear and, often, requiring government and social benefits.

All of this, along with other socioeconomic factors, accounts for the high numbers of migrants requiring social benefits to get by—generation after generation.

***

I am of the opinion that these socioeconomic problems could be slowed and resolved.

A government worker at the job center once told me of her experience with the marginalization of foreigners on the job or in the job training markets. As she narrated her stories to me, she couldn't quite hold back her tears. I could not help sharing tears too.

She told me about two young men who had just graduated from the secondary school and wanted to learn a profession. One of them was the child of an immigrant from Iraq, and the other was an ethnic German.

Both hoped to become auto mechanics, and both were vying for a position in a shop so they could complete their practicals. The immigrant's child had better grades than did the ethnic German. However, while the ethnic German had many workshops offering him a place to work on his practical skills, the immigrants child was always turned down by the workshops he applied to.

The woman who told me the story was furious. She went with this young man to four different companies, campaigning and canvassing on his behalf. She would ask, "What is wrong with this young man? He has the best grades. He looks good. Why is it that you won't accept him and give him a place to prove himself?" She assured me there was no reason other than his ethnicity that this young man was being denied. She added that, while a lot of integration of foreigners is going on in the public realm, privately, nothing has changed.

As she narrated her story, my eyes filled with tears. Here was a German confirming to me the true picture of the society we live in. We are all human beings. We all have feelings and dignity. No one wants to be treated like a "no man." Many years ago, in the United States Declaration of Independence, Thomas Jefferson said, "We hold this truth to be self evident, that all men are created equal, that they are endowed by their creator with certain unalienable Rights, that among these are Life, Liberty, and the pursuit of Happiness." He said this with the vision of living this principles to its truest meanings and sharing it with others. A society can actually realize God's own dream for humankind—the dream that existed before human beings so much as thought of turning the world into an ocean of lies and deceit.

There is still no country in the world today other than the United States where people who are not living in their country of birth can realize their dreams. And yet they do it in spite of numerous challenges, like racial prejudice, which will plague humanity as long as human beings exist.

Many people have migrated from as far away as Bombay, Abeokuta, Tacloban, Zungeru, and all corners of the earth and made the United States their home. They have done so with full confidence in the protection, opportunity, and freedoms that are rare commodities in their native countries.

Some even take these things for granted saying, "America is a no-man's land." Yes it is, but visionaries fought for the execution of policies by various American presidents that make possible advancements like the Civil Rights Movement. Such movements give way to the belief in fairness by the people of the United States, which makes dreams come true, in spite of numerous challenges in race relations.

When Clarence Thomas, a black judge, was appointed by the senior George Bush to the Supreme Court of the land in the nineties, I was in Japan. As he said, "Only in America could this day be possible." More than twenty years later, I am still fascinated by not only the person who shared this quote but also by the person who made this quote in the first case.

***

I have even seen people of color who came to the United States, say twenty years ago from Asia, calling on the American people to reinstate the Jim Crow systems because they now live in freedom and enjoy the benefits of the civil rights movement. Martin Luther,

John Lewis, and Rosa Park, among others, fought for important changes. I am impressed with the way black people in the United States have been able to make use of the rights their forefathers fought and died for.

But I am afraid of the fact that these opportunities have not been fully utilized by black Americans. Others are just eating away their lunch. For example, some come from other lands and see the freedom and opportunity. They seize it and, having grabbed hold of it for themselves, move to white neighborhoods. Some who are dark but have straight hairs even begin to see themselves as whites and, when they sees a black man on the street, they call him an African or an African American.

Now in my own opinion black Americans should never use the term or allow anyone of any race to call them African Americans. That's incorrect terminology. The hidden agenda behind that term African American is a reminder of the force that was used to take many people away from their original homes. And that's denigrating. They never came in search of the new world or wealth or fame or freedom. Rather, they were forced against their will and were treated unkindly. If you were born in the United States and anyone calls you African American, just resist it. You are an American, and that's okay.

When the first settlers came to Jamestown, little did they know that life was going to be difficult. But they were determined to push on with their missions, and they accomplished it. To this day, let's be frank without any bias, if the white people or the European Americans do not have the advantages they have today, then they have not done better. They came in first. That's the fact that must be recognized and respected. Having said that, black people must be seen as equal, able partners and should not be viewed with automatic suspicion.

Hatred is not what built America. America was built on freedoms and based on shared dreams of her people and generosity. Hatred doesn't build; it destroys. So let's all work together. These days the younger generations of politicians are allowing the powers of politics to break the necks of the dreams upon which America has been built by undermining or not respecting the will of the people.

By creating an atmosphere of divisions within the system, you are indirectly telling the world that your house can no longer sustain the challenges of the test of time. I am not suggesting but appealing to everyone—gay people, lesbians, straight people, boys, girls, old people, young people, black people, Indians, Asians, Tibetan, pastors, and priests, Buddhists—embrace the policy of acceptance.

That word *tolerance* still has a lot of biased reservations. It must not be used when we are embracing each other as human beings. We must learn to *accept* each other. After all, the world belongs to us all—to the rich and the poor, the wicked and the generous. We all have a common goal—to live and die. And death knows no man.

When children are born, they know no hate. Rather, influences around them—primarily influences of adults—make them to think and act the way they do.

An America president once said, "No problem of human making is too great to be overcome by human ingenuity, human energy, and the untiring hope of the human spirit." I am fascinated with this land of hope and generosity and with their presidents.

Don't tell me God doesn't endorse who the next president of America will be. He knows, because, if America doesn't take the right steps, no one else will.

7

It profits no one to continue to deny people their dreams. If you have doubts about all I have been saying, please take some time go to the Frankfurt Airport at night. Visit the cargo sections, and you will see fork lifters and loaders in the hundreds. Who is operating this machinery? You'll find that 90 percent of these laborers are foreigners. Go to the warehouses. Who will you find? Again, you will see a vast majority of the warehouse workers are foreigners.

Now wait between 7:45 a.m. and 8:00 a.m. Then you will see, in the same warehouses and cargo offices, Germans coming in the hundreds—men and women with well-combed hair, dazzling neckties, well-ironed shirts and creased pants, evenly cut fingernails.

Don't immigrants and their children deserve such dignified jobs as well? Everyone owns what he or she earns. But there is foul play if everyone does not have access to equal opportunity.

In the world we live in, there will always be differences in humans. But it is not a crime to give every child that golden opportunity in life to exhale, especially in a civilized and prosperous society like Germany. In this country, education is free. Yet go to the campuses, you will find scanty students with migrant backgrounds.

Few foreigners, perhaps .05 percent of them, hold dignified jobs. In a population of about eighty-two million people, visit institutions such as universities or organizations like the police, the banks, and law offices, and you will see the disparity. Look into who are the CEOs of companies; you will not find anyone with a migrant history or background.

In my twenty years of living in Germany, I have never seen a black police officer. There are some Turkish police officers, but their guns are without bullets, and they do not play any relevant roles in decision-making process.

Immigrants or foreigners who do hold positions in these institutions and organizations are always assistants. That's the highest position any immigrant can occupy in "morgen rot land." There are some politicians with migrant backgrounds who are there as alibis of integration in politics. Well, it's all "croco" integrations.

***

A few years ago, I read about Colin Powell's book *My Way*. In it, I read about America's support for the real, true integration of her people in its American dream beliefs as defined by the fundamentals of the founding fathers.

The book explains in literal terms the difficulty one sometimes faces in Germany if your skin is black or brown or if you are not a "biological German." On page 361, the general narrates the accident his son, Mike Powell, had while stationed in Germany as a soldier with the US Army. He describes how a doctor in a German hospital reacted to his son. The doctor in charge said, "Für den da können wir nicht mehr tun" (We can do no more). Lieutenant Brechtbuhl jumped from his examination table and said, "You can't give up on him. I want you to call an American hospital now." As I write this, I am overcome with emotions, not because of the doctor, but because of Lieutenant Brechtbuhl, who saved Mike's life. As a father, I can relate to Colin Powell's experience.

The doctor's phrase "den da" is used to talk about something that is low quality or is not needed. Upon hearing the phrase, Lieutenant

Brechtbuhl simply said, "Sie durfen ihn nicht aufgeben" (Don't give up on him). He knew the doctor was about to leave Mike to die.

This is the reality—outright judgments on anything not considered German. This is how the dreams of children are being wasted every day. Year in year out, they are not taken seriously.

***

James Madison, an American president, once said, "The advancement and diffusion of knowledge is the only guardian of true liberty." Think about it. You are hiding the instruments of knowledge from some who were born and bred in the same society as were your children. It will only be a matter of time before the systems collapses.

Every day, one hears things like, "We need well-educated immigrants in Germany. They should first have a professions in their native countries before they are given visas to come to Germany." Such announcements are made on radio broadcasts and in television programs. I've even heard people say we should have migration systems similar to those of Canada, Australia, or the United States.

These are countries on different continents and with different mentalities. In Canada, for example, many issues are solved through decision making. In Europe, the situation is complicated, as history is always revisited. Europeans have, for too long, been at the mercy of wars and tyranny—subject to the control of empires, among them the Ottomans and the Habsburgs. Too many adversaries, too many suspicions, and too much hatred has filled the pages of Europe's history books. This has fostered the belief that anything that is foreign should be viewed with suspicion and the hesitancy to talk of too many bothers. Germany would have to develop its own concepts of migration within the framework of its mentality, culture, and perceptions.

An American president once said that no problems of human nature cannot be overcome or solved. George Washington had the opportunity to proclaim himself king or emperor of America. But for the sake of freedom and democracy, he declined.

If he had been a European, things would have gone the other way. So copying migration systems from North America would not work in Germany.

***

I have some ideas on how the migration difficulties could be laid out so as to solve the problems migrants are facing in Germany, as well as what migrants themselves must undertake in order to move on with their lives here in Germany.

Here are some of my perspectives. The German society would have to embrace people without suspicions, starting as early as kindergarten. People would have to learn not to treat German children preferentially and to respect all children, no matter their race, color, or religion. To me, that means implementing child laws that ensure each child's individual needs are considered—that each child's perceptions about life and dreams should be explored, not undermined or ignored.

The encouragement of children in their own world is important. I heard my children say things like *Deutsche kinder*—phrases indicating preference for German children they likely heard from their tutors. All children are children and should be protected from "hate sermons" by the few who pretend to the outside world to accept people but are yet to accept the simple truth about life in its simplicity and complications.

We all have a share in this world. Either we are part of the problem or we are part of the solution. Being part of the solution would be the ultimate option. We all need someone. How can a queen or a king be a queen or a king without subjects? How can you tell what is endowed in a child without helping him or her to unlock it? How can you judge people according to their color, their religion, or their sexual orientation?

Who has made any man or woman a judge? What right has anyone anywhere to determine where humans like himself or herself are to be placed? There are two possibilities when it comes to people who see people and then judge them. Either they are lying and don't want to see the truth, or they are deceiving themselves or living in a world that is absolutely wrapped in fantasies.

The government of this country has a role to play toward the proper integrations of foreigners. It must stress the benefits to everyone if foreigners are willingly given the opportunity to unlock their potential.

Migrants and migrants' children should not be seen as burdens or exploiters of the social systems. Some measures toward a proper integration of migrants already in place. However, elements of prejudgments by those charged with implementing them have held back of their implementation.

There should be more open discussions on integration. This has to involve more than people simply reading books that support the conclusions they have already come to and repeating what they have read to the media.

I believe the problem with us as humans in general lies not with what we already know or what was said long ago by someone somewhere but, rather, with things we do not know and the challenge of how to come by new knowledge and then cherish it.

Mandatory new skills requirements should be put in place to address the issue of migrants with long histories of unemployment. Anyone who has been unemployed for more than one year should be required to learn a skill of his or her choice. The structures to do so are already in place, so implementing such a program would not be overly costly for the government.

In the current system, unemployed people in Germany are given health services, housing, food, and so on because Germany is a socialist state. Many unemployed people today have been living on social welfare benefits (Hartz IV) for more than five years. Some are passing this situation on to their children. There is something wrong with the system.

Moreover, there should be some kind of sanctions against those who are not willing to learn new skills.

The German language should be designed specifically for job trainings for older immigrants having difficulties with securing a job. They should be made to understand that there is no easy ride in life, no matter what one does.

Policies are not mentality, so when the government wants to make policies to accommodate and integrate migrants, the people should be involved. The government must sell the advantages of truly integrating immigrants into the society. Those in authority must tell the German people that their own security can only be fully guaranteed when people of different nations are well integrated in the society. They must help people understand that when did people leave their countries to come and stay in a country, its an indication of that's country's progress and development.

Politicians must stop spreading fear among the people with the sole intention of winning elections at the detriments of migrants.

Integrated foreigners should be required to teach other foreigners the German language. Those who have learned the language themselves will have a better grasp of the simplest method for understanding the basics of the German language. German is simple and easy to learn, if one understands the connections between the basics and the components in the spoken words.

***

Foreigners or migrants, on their part, should be made to understand that social welfare was not designed to be passed from generation to generation by its recipients. Rather, it is intended to help people who have lost their jobs or who are experiencing some difficulties in life until they are able to find a new job.

Social benefits should not be a way of life. Social benefits can only render people isolated, stifling their dreams. The money you get from the state is only for rent and food. It doesn't make you to be productive. Anyone relying on these benefits as a means of living should think about the negative effects doing so has on one's life.

For example, a recent study shows that children from homes with families living on social benefits do not perform as well in schools as children from homes with regular incomes. Children of families living on social welfare are more likely to go to schools in hotspot quarters with lower quality education programs than those attended by children from well-situated families.

Besides, people living on social benefits are often called *azozial*, a term used to describe someone who depends largely on others for existence.

Having said all this, the key for anyone to be productive in any given society is to feel as if he or she is a part of the society. In his or her heart, a person must feel included.

Many ideas about the proper integration of migrants have failed because the authorities who ought to implement them in schools, in offices, and in other places throughout society have failed to see migrants the way they themselves would like to be seen and treated.

True survival of knowledge and prosperity will not come by preventing certain people in a society from acquiring knowledge but, rather, from ensuring that it is passed to all those who are willing to embrace it and spread it for the betterment of society, regardless of race, religion, sex, or sexual orientation.

James Madison recognized this fact many years ago when he said, "The advancement and diffusion of knowledge is the only guardian of true liberty."

Let everyone having doubts about migrants' contribution to society give them true opportunities to explore and discover themselves as endowed by their creator. Then wait and let the results speaks for themselves.

***

Demographic changes have now made it almost impossible to avert full integration of migrants. I was recently at an interview with twelve other people. Each and everyone of us, save one German, had a migrant background. That's the reality here, and no one should pretend that this demographic situation does not exist or ignore this simple fact.

Trying to lure professional migrants from their countries of origin by way of cheap visa programs is not going to solve the problem. Rather, the lack of integration of foreigners in Germany is the key problem when it comes to the lack of professionals in the key sectors of the economy.

Many professionals would like to look somewhere else, were there are better integration systems and where they are taken seriously and given the freedom to express and explore themselves in their own terms.

Proper integration systems would do the jobs. Not having a system that leaves migrants with no better option than the road that leads to nowhere (in the form of social welfare) is the key. It costs society more to recruit young men and women into welfare benefit schemes than it would to recruit them into professional and fulfilled lives.

***

Having written about these psychological discriminations and their effects on the German society, I believe there is hope. I believe that things could be reversed in the positive direction. A new approach toward migrants is needed.

President Lyndon B. Johnson who once said, "There is a clear river and a bad river that must flow together to one direction."

Think of the Turkish father who was determined that his son would obtain a university degree. Think of Otto Bismarck, who made health insurance available to all in Germany. Think of Wolfgang Schäuble, the German finance minister who knew how to implement plans and how to convince people to agree to his plans. He told people what they did not want to hear and spoke of what they were afraid of. Think of my father, who said, "When everyone is looking to the sky for help, you look to the ground for help, because, in it, grows everything you need to survive. And when you die, you will return to it again." All of these examples give me hope that, one day, migrants and their children will be given the opportunity of their lives.

Germany is an inheritance land. The wealth of many of her citizens is wealth that has been passed from generation to generation. The problem with this kind of wealth is that it doesn't create room for people to innovate properly. Rather, too many cling tightly to traditions.

How about those children, both foreigners and ethnic Germans, whose parents are not rich or who do not have the prospect of inheriting properties? The only way they can survive is to explore their natural abilities, which were endowed upon them by God.

In life, we all have a plan. No human being lives without a plan for how to survive. Life brings both extremely difficult experiences and beautiful passages.

Let everyone take a moment and look at our natural world— our landscapes, our seas and our oceans, the animals. Are they not beautiful? All we need can be found in nature. Take, for example, the night and the day. They each have their rules. They respect each other, and they have their time.

I am not afraid of the things I know, but I have respect for the things I do not know. When the night comes and we are asleep, we do not even know our names, and this applies to queens and kings and everything living. In dreams, we become something supernatural. We can be anywhere, and sometimes dreams do comes true.

8

THE DAY WE WERE BORN is not important. The day we die is also not important. But the days in between—these days are important. What we do today can affect people after us. No matter who you are, were you live, what color your skin is, what religion you practice, or whether you are a man or a woman, your actions affect others. I want you, when you stand up in the morning, to say to yourself I want to be an inclusive person.

I don't want you to be too kind or too generous. But be inclusive in your judgments, and you'll soon find out that people want to be around you.

We all need someone. Someone gave birth to us. Someone is going to take us to the cemetery when we are gone.

In January 2005, new reformations of the social laws and job improvement initiatives were born to tackle the massive unemployment rates in Germany at the time. Under these laws, the unemployment benefits and the social welfare supports were joined together as one entity. This new law was named after the commission chairman, Peter Hartz. With the various amendments, it was dubbed the Hartz IV. Under Hartz IV, one can only be qualified for unemployment benefits for a year. Thereafter, one must go to the second department of the job office known as the job center.

At the job center, one is guaranteed fundamental security needs, like housing and food, one so long as he or she doesn't have a job or income. This is state's effort to defend and deliver its promise as a social welfare state. With more than four million employees, the social industry is one of the highest employers in Germany.

At the job center, one becomes a recipient of "*arbeitlosengeld II*" (unemployment money II). The 2 means you have exceeded the unemployment benefits, which last for a year. You are now practically on welfare.

Here is the problem with the job center and its goals and objectives. I would call arbeitlosengeld II a control instrument. It further brings confusion and uncertainty to the minds of its recipients and further impoverishes those who are already watching society from the sidelines.

Hartz IV is a symbol of poverty and the absolute dehumanization of humans. It makes people stop thinking on their own, waiting, rather, for the state to provide practically everything, like dogs waiting for food and commands from their masters. Recipients are considered to be on the bottom rungs of society's ladder. To many who have never tasted poverty, they are thought of as parasites, lazy people who are living from the sweat of others.

And once you are in the system, the road to working a normal job becomes a question of survival and struggle. Many have given up hope and turned to drinking away their troubles. Many feel helpless. The children of Hartz IV recipients are the most vulnerable—the most likely to become school dropouts, to get pregnant as teenagers, and to be relegated to the lowest schools in Germany. Above all, they are likely to end up like their parents, dependent on the same Hartz IV system they where born into.

And if they themselves are not careful enough, their own children will ultimately end up in the same situation. It is neither uncommon nor surprising that few ethnic Germans and many foreigners are living on social welfare—in third generations.

***

One should not be quick to point to the caste system in India. A caste system actually exists in Germany. It exists unnoticed because it doesn't have the backings of any religious sentiments. Otherwise, it would be more obvious.

In Germany, for example, your family background and the financial capacity of your parents ultimately determine your educational aspirations and career. Your surname and skin colors are also factors that determine your success in life here in Germany.

About 36,960 Lebanese people are living in Germany; a shocking 33,424 (90 percent) are living on Hartz IV. The situation is not any better among other ethnic minority groups. Why these alarming numbers? That is exactly the purpose of *Paper German*; it is intended to explain the systems, which I have witnessed over the last twenty years of my life, that have led to these circumstances.

Many Lebanese came to Germany as refugees and were never allowed to work. Those who did work did so illegally. This lifestyle was passed on from generation to generation. The other factor is that the Lebanese population in Germany has not been well equipped educationally. Tell me, how can you be educationally equipped when you cannot work or mingle with the ethnic Germans? Where are you going to get the necessary language skills to drive you further? What happens is that you have first and then second generations living on social welfare benefits.

To many, this is now a way of life. The adverse effects of this situation are often underestimated, thus creating a larger cleft between the haves and the have-nots. Even within the have-nots there is further stratification. Those considered underneath the have-nots are often referred to *Hartz IV empfänger*. These Hartz IV beneficiaries are mostly foreigners. Why is it mostly foreigners who are receiving these pills of self-destruction? The answer is not far-fetched. There is a ripple effect in the society that makes it difficult or impossible to elevate oneself from poverty.

Foreigners tend to end up with low educational qualifications, which is brought about by a lack of acceptance of their abilities in the society that they have chosen. They are not morally supported by those who ought to help them see the opportunities in their lives.

Many are reluctant to even attempt to pursue an education or professional careers because they don't see any meaningful avenues of engaging in a venture or of receiving recognition by the German society. Even if they do pursue an education, if they are not careful, they might well end up in the hands of unserious jobs consultant companies, exploiting their talents for a while and then dumping them like a refuge in the hands of job centers.

Because they do not posses educational qualifications, they are not employed by anyone. This is a clear argument not to employ anyone. But let's see the real situations. Were they given the opportunity to educate themselves? Were they ever given a chances at even the lowest level? Of course not.

Three of four migrants have no profession, and the one that does is discriminated against in the employment markets. If there is crisis in the company, the first to go is the migrant, so there is virtually no chance at all for foreigners or migrants in Germany.

***

There are children who were born and bred here. This is the only country they have ever known, and German is the only language they understand and cherish. But while their land may be Germany, they are still considered foreigners—still discriminated against—because of their appearance, their skin color, or their religion. The members of this generation, unlike their parents—who struggled and assimilated, aware that psychological discriminations were a way of life—are sensitive and cautious of their environs.

How do you convince a society that still reads the story of *Hänsel und Gretel* to children—the story of a stepmother who asked her husband to send his children away into the bush so that they themselves would have enough to eat—that we must consider the needs of others?

The children wanted to be with their father and no one else. Twice, they where dumped in the bush and made their way home because one of the children cleverly dropped first bread crumbs and then stones on the way to the forest.

The story ended with the children reuniting with their father after the death of their stepmother. They brought with them some riches from a witch they encountered in the course of their wanderings in the forest. They killed the witch and took her riches home to their father.

No story could better explain the intolerant nature of a society that has gained so much from others, especially the United States of America after the Second World War, than this children's book, still loved and cherished by parents all across Germany. The book alludes to injustice going and poverty, as the children were born to a peasant—a woodcutter. These two factors—poverty and injustice—tend to make Germans behave strangely toward things they ought to love and cherish and understand.

The Marshall Plan actually acted as a stimulant to rebuild Germany after the two world wars. The airdrops by the French and English governments helped as well. But these days, little is said of those helping hands that brought Germany out of its ruins.

These days, a popular TV station continues to show Hitler and his men, his weapons and his technological drives. The station shows his drives for success—how he built roads and bridges and planes and submarines—and the killings that were carried out on an unimaginable scale and the church, who favored the executions of Jewish people.

I have never seen a single mention on those programs of those who helped rebuild Germany. Sometimes, I have heard older people saying they rebuilt this country by themselves after the wars, so we do not need these *kanakes* (a term Germans often use for the people of Poland). It's always *wir Deutsche* (we Germans) or *nur Deutsche* (only Germans). All others are somewhat inferior, counterfeit, not deserving of being seen.

In life, there is enough for everyone. If only we could see and appreciate things that do not look like us. But then they are all there.

***

A friend once asked her Christian colleague about the possibility of studying to become a nurse in Germany.

Her colleague's reply was "You'd better go for cleaning. It's easier, no qualifications are required, and you'll be earning money."

But is cleaning the only thing a person who is not a German can do? What are the reasons behind this kind of indirect hostility toward foreigners?

The reasons are to be found not only in the individual people but also in the society as a whole. There is a bridge between the family and the community. There is a broader sense of community among the Germans when it comes to isolation of foreigners, in terms of jobs, as well as in social, cultural, and political arenas.

***

A few years ago, I took a vacation to Spain—to the Playa de las Americas, to be precise. I went to the nightclubs to dance, together with my wife, and we got to know two very friendly women from Germany. On one occasion, we even hung out and did some outdoor activities together, and we were all happy.

After two weeks, we drove on the same bus to the airport and eventually took the same plane back to Germany. While in the plane, we learned that they live and work in the same city we live in. To me, a friendship between us had been established, so I was already thinking about our next activity once we were back in Germany. To my greatest disappointment and surprise, when I drew out my address book to enter their contacts as the bus that had brought us to Freiburg came to a halt, one of the women said simply, "Man sieht sich wieder auf zufall" (We will meet by chance). Immediately, they both exited. That was the last I ever saw of the two women, who had been very friendly in another land but were very unfriendly the moment their feet stepped on German soil.

To my wife, this was no surprise. She had once told me, "There are those who only talk to you because you are black, not necessarily because they are generally interested in you. They want to know what you are doing, where you are going, and how long you are going to stay in Germany. In Germany, this is called *plump neugier* (sarcastic inquisitiveness). Don't be too surprised if you live in Germany for a very long time in and yet you do not have a German friend. Germans are typically not open to foreigners.

This is due to the long poverty that existed. Remember the story of Hänsel and Gretel. The source of injustice needs to be destroyed. The two children were clever to return home with stolen jewels from the witch. This represents the celebration of the German courage. After their ultimate triumph against the witch, they returned to their father, whom they loved very much, and they were very happy with their father.

Now take a closer look at this story. We have a father who was willing to dump his children in the bush simply because his wife said there wasn't enough food for all. He never took the time to think about his actions. He simply agreed, even when he knew his children had no one else and that they were certainly going to die of hunger in the bush or be killed by some wild animals.

Because he was not willing to confront his wife or didn't want to be seen as offending his wife, who was not the mother of those little children, he simply agreed to carry out that kind of thoughtless act.

***

Today, the silent discriminations going on are simply ignored, and everyone is pretending as if everything is well and that foreigners are well taken care of and well situated.

No one talks about the hidden denials faced by foreigners and their children. Even when someone takes the courage to say something, he or she is not taken seriously or simply ignored. Some might even deem an individual who speaks out *verräter des vaterland* (traitor of our fatherland). This might not be said publicly, but in the minds of many, it is the right phrase to describe anyone trying to bring light to this darkness.

A great deal of hostility against foreigners is prevalent in our society. Yet the perpetrators are hardly made to face the law. They run around freely burning homes for asylum seekers and abusing and beating up of foreigners, especially in the eastern part of the country.

Some perpetrators went so far as to threaten the life of a mayor of a major city in the east and those of his family members for building shelters to house asylum seekers. The mayor was forced to resign as a result of the death threats. Racially intolerant parties are sitting in parliaments, and judges with neo-Nazi affinities presiding over jurisdictions.

The government of the day is watching as all of these things unfold—as society moves again in the direction of the "program nachts." The only difference is that, these days, it's not Jews but Muslims and foreigners that are being singled out. The reason the situation has not gotten out of hand is that there are jobs for Germans who want to work. People can see the evidence that foreigners and migrants are not competing with them and taking away their jobs.

Foreigners, unlike the Jews who had substantial assets, have nothing to be taken or robbed from them. I read sometime ago that even the golden fillings in Jewish teeth were targeted and that many Jews lost their lives because of the gold in their mouths.

Foreigners have nothing. They are all simply existing, not actually living, and the German society knows that.

I have heard and read on the advertisements in stations and on the bus their slogan for dealing with the situation: "Lass uns Ausländer tolerieren" (Let's tolerate foreigners). This is dangerous. It insinuates that we (the Germans) are the clever and wise ones. We are providing help to foreigners. We are the real people. They (the foreigners) have nothing. Don't be afraid of them. This slogan is designed to diffuse the psychologically tense situation existing in everyday life here for migrants.

But with this kind of slogan, there is no alternative to the current situation—no move toward properly integrating migrants and foreigners into the society, no acknowledgment of the demographic situation confronting Germany and much of the Western world.

If the social *vertrag* (contract) is going to be made sustainable, then the society and the state must change its attitude toward migrants and foreigners. This is not going to be an easy task, but the time to rewrite history for the good is now.

***

It is never too late to make a change. There is still hope, which is the cornerstone of change.

I am optimistic because the younger generations of Germans are much more open and aware of the dangers of the old ways. They are clever kids, and they have been able to detect the lies they have been told by the older generations.

Here in Germany, there is a kind of generational conflict between the younger generations and the older generations. The latter still see wars as the only solution to every conflict. The former feel they are being carried around by their elders like little babies and seem to be asking the question, when on earth are you going to allow us to decide for ourselves which way to go?

Here is a typical example of this generational conflict. Take a doctor, say, with his own clinic or a little practice or doctor's office. He would do everything possible to encourage his son or daughter to follow in his footsteps by becoming a doctor as well. Or similarly, a manager in a company would also encourage his children to work for the same company he works for. The list could go on and on. The point is, on the one hand, the parents are trying to create an opportunity for their children, which is a good thing. But the other side of the coin is that there is no room for innovation. There is also no room for creativity. By assuring a child that he or she already has a place in your own place of work, as a parent you create a situation where the child doesn't actually think anymore about big dreams. He or she now thinks, in accordance with human psychology, *I am through already with the stress of finding a job. I only need to get some good grades. Even if I don't have good grades, success is assured.* The child already knows that he or she will work at his mother's place of work or take over her father's medical practice when he retires.

The structure keeps business and success in the family, but it can only work for some time. In a longer-term perspective, it is not sustainable. These days, the world is like a global village. Everybody, with suitcases in hand, is looking for opportunities everywhere. If you don't change your ways, change will take you by surprise, and the cost of change becomes more expensive.

This system leaves no room for innovation. Young people are forced to take a path that has already been paved, and those with other ideas or proclivities toward other fields are indirectly discouraged.

If this kind of resistance to change continues, it's only a matter of time before the next conflict will arise. Germans do not like to take a seat at the back, preferring instead to be at the front. In order to stay in front and stay competitive, some kind of compromise must be made.

These measures must include the unconditional integration of migrants and foreigners. Otherwise, Germany might become a ghost town, with empty houses and apartments and school and kindergarten closures, and what will remain will be the weak and the old.

These kinds of conditions already exist in the eastern part of the country. If the current trend of indirectly restricting foreigners to positions as garbage collectors, cleaners, and dishwashers continues, very soon the ghost town will set its feet in the western part of the country as well.

I think it was a minister from Uzbekistan who once said, "Every time I am on tour in Germany, I always expect to see a young, dynamic person of my age, but to my greatest surprise, they are always old people, who cannot really understands the principle of dynamism as related to the modern times." This is very true. The older generations are not willing to give up entitlements, but the reality is that everything must change. The young become old, and somehow we all need to come to the conclusion that life is not eternal and cannot be treated as such.

9

IT WAS ENLIGHTENMENT BROUGHT ABOUT by Francis Bacon, Copernicus, Columbus, and Martin Luther that helped shape Europe and make it the most powerful continent on earth. But toward the end of the nineteenth century, between 1915 and 1945, to be precise, nearly one hundred million people were dead because of wars and starvation. At the heights of these successes, a country as small as Belgium was controlling the Congo, the Netherlands was controlling some parts of Indonesia, and Europe was controlling more than forty million square kilometers, with Britain controlling more than half of these territories.

These enlightenments—based on viewing nature, interpreting what it had to offer, and challenging it for some practical solutions to human challenges—brought progress. The Industrial Revolution was the indirect result of studying nature, as was the direction of the priest who believed that you could serve your God yourself without having to go through the priest. Before 1446 (before the first printing press was invented), people would wait for the priest to tell them about God every Sunday. But after the invention of the printing press, people could read the Bible on their own without priests and other ecclesiastical leaders acting and pretending to be acting in the name of the Lord.

***

Putting this in relationship to the modern-day foreigners in Germany, Germans should not be afraid of foreigners or see them as a threat to their national pride or the security of their country. All the foreigners want is a sense of inclusion, not exclusion.

Let society try to get the best out of people by not only looking at and reducing them to their skin colors or their religion or their sexual orientation.

It is sad to know that my daughter can never serve in the Deutsche Army, simply because she is black. My sons can never serve on the police force or in the army, simply because they are of mixed race. They will have a hard time getting a job as a banker.

I once asked a friend in the nineties, "Du Harald sag mal wurdest du mich dein Geld geben, wenn ich irgendwo auf der bank arbeitet und du als kunden?" (Harald, would you give me your money if I happened to work at the counter in a bank and you were the customer?).

He replied, "Soll ich dir anlügen oder die wahrheit sagen?" (Should I tell you the truth or lie to you?).

I told him I wanted him to tell me the truth.

His reply was that he would rather prefer to see a German behind the bank counter and no one else.

This illustrates the views held by the vast majority of the populace when it comes to foreigners working in public places or having a job considered to be for the Germans.

I remember seeing how a black woman who was working at a counter in a supermarket was deliberately abused. I almost spilled tears as I watched and old woman shouting at her about what she considered not right in her receipt. Two weeks later, I went to the same supermarket. The woman was no longer on the counter but somewhere else.

***

The harsh conditions in the job markets that migrants in Germany face are echoed in the social arena. Foreigners face difficulties when it comes to financial transactions. For instance, renting homes or apartments can be tricky. A large majority of migrants live in council flats and in apartments Germans themselves would never live in. In these kinds of apartments, the owners are always very friendly.

If you are buying anything as a foreigner and the German you're dealing with is very friendly to you, keeps calling to ask where you are, or shows concern about you, be very skeptical. Never rush to acquire such items. If the items being sold are of good quality, the seller will never call or show concern about your whereabouts. That's just the simple truth. This not about someone being wicked or racist. It's just the nature of Germans.

If you are a foreigner and want to sell something, say a used car, to a German, you will likely hear the following questions: Are you the real owner of this car? How long have you been in possession of it? What is your bottom-line price? How long have you been in Germany?

The prospective buyer may comment on how well you can speak German or note that this is Germany, in Germany *bei uns* (by us or here in Germany).

This small talk is designed to make you feel that what you are about to sell is not worth much and an attempt to cut down the price. These are the hidden facts behind these questions, which might not be known to someone new in Germany.

***

I have observed many little things in my two decades of living and working here in Germany. Germans are quite sensitive to humiliation. However, they themselves are keen to be a party to the humiliation of others.

I have often deliberately asked my colleagues about who won the World Cup of 1998 (the French won). Here is what I have learned. If the Germans won, it's always, "Peter, have you seen the match yesterday? Ha ha! Deutschland." If they lost, I will go and ask them if they saw the match, and they will tell me, "I was so tired, I went to bed early. I did not watch the game."

How can you believe a German going to bed when the German team is playing? The reason is clear. The Germans cannot accept defeat as an option and never have an easy time convincing themselves to accept that sometimes one needs to condole a loss. Hence, they have an incredible hard time accepting people who do not look like them.

Germans simply believe that, if you want to be integrated into society, that's your own problem. You came to our country, they believe; how you live is your own problem. We are not ready to make any compromise as far as our perceptions of you as a foreigner, and the opportunities here are only for Germans. If you don't like it, pack your bags and go.

This is the indirect attitude of the populace. The government is doing all it can to open up its society via various integration programs *beauftragte der bundesregierung* (instructed by the federal government). These are all forwarded by television organizations, often occupied by people who do not know the common man on the streets, his needs, or his well-being.

***

The integrations of newcomers into any given society is not one-sided but, rather, a symbiotic relationship between the guests and the host.

You can only get the best of anybody if you accept him or her with open arms. Only then will true integration follow. Different societies have their own ways of life and, so, different ways to address the long hurdles of integrations are needed in different societies around the globe.

The integration system in Canada, for example, could never work in Australia or Great Britain or the United States or Germany. These are all different nations with different mentalities and different views about life.

Maybe they could learn from each other, but they still need consider their unique cultural values and ways of life. These aspects of a society are very important when it comes to successfully integrating migrants.

I keep hearing the phrase "Western values," and it's often used when referring to developed nations. What are these values? And who sets them? You cannot used the term *Western values* to represent the general opinions of different nations who, through industrial revolutions, had similarities but with different identities deeply rooted in their various cultures.

In Germany, for example, before Christianity was introduced, the Germans where actually pagans, and some of the pagan influence can still be seen to this days. Christianity actually suppressed their appetite for blood, so one cannot say they have the same values as Canadians or Australians.

We should all believe in differentiations and embrace appreciation and utmost respect for our differences. Only when we respect and appreciate each other can we fully integrate with one another.

The integration of migrants and their children is not the sole responsibility of the migrants alone. It is a societal issue that must be addressed in the most humble and truthful manner. Ignore the problems and pretend that nothing is happening is dangerous.

Flocks of refugees have come to Germany in recent times. But what has become of them? Are there any success stories that tell of an immigrant becoming, say, a doctor or a well-known singer or a member of the police force? I don't know of any or of any migrants who have been encouraged to seek these kinds of successes.

There is an outright embargo on migrants and even Germans who are born and bred in Germany but whose names are not Müller or Schwarzkopf or Burkart or Textor. If you are not one of the chosen few, you can never be given a chance to rise and shine the way God wants you to.

If you have to reduce everyone who is not German to taking mediocre jobs, indirectly denying them the opportunity to so much as acquire the right education for professional careers, and forcing the vast majority of them to end up receiving Hartz IV, then the next crises is already on its way.

Giving human beings opportunities to shine actually benefits not only those who are in need of those opportunities, but those who are giving them as well. I am fascinated by the story of Jan Koum, who came to the United States all the way from Ukraine in 1992. By the ending of 2014, he was a billionaire. His story fascinates me because it demonstrates how humans can do some extraordinary things if given opportunities and the chance to express themselves.

Koum moved from Ukraine with his mother and grandmother, and with the help of a welfare program, the three shared a two-bedroom apartment. His mother worked as a babysitter, and he worked as a cleaner in a grocery store. But he had the opportunity to educate himself.

He went on to found the social network app WhatsApp, which is now been used around the world. That eventually made him a billionaire within two decades of his arrival in the United States. A man who once lived on food stamps, today, thanks to the encouragement and the supports he got from his new home, could now feed an entire town for generations if he so wished. There is a message in this wonderful story: Hard work alone cannot guarantee success. You need opportunities within the framework of whatever society or country you live in in order to thrive.

***

I have never seen any lazy foreigner in Germany who does not like to work, but society makes people frustrated, and frustrations can lead to laziness. A society that is based on and concerned with the welfare of only the ethnic majority and is hostile to the minority cannot sustain the future, even when it seems the contributions of the minorities does not counts.

The social welfare in Germany is a one-sided system, which does not in anyway encourage its recipients to take actions to elevate themselves out of their situations. I have my own reasons for intending this belief. I have lived this social welfare system, and I am a witness to how it works and operates.

If you go to the welfare stations known as job center in the morning, say 9:00 a.m., you will find the entire hall filled with people. Watch closely, and you will see only elderly Germans or alcoholic Germans or disabled Germans among the crowd. Every other person you'll find will be young and vibrant, with qualifications, and willing to work. These people will have been searching for jobs for many years. They will have no other means of living, save a resorting to taking this welfare in order to survive.

Now take a closer look at these young, vibrant people. They are migrants or Germans with Turkish roots or black people or Eastern Europeans or Indians. This is the bitter balance of a society pretending to be honest with foreigners and yet hostile to them.

All the workers in this job center are Germans. You will never find a foreigner among them. Most of them are in their retirement ages, still clinging to their jobs as if glued to them. Sometime nature is going to intervene, but before then the damage will have been done—the opportunities they greedily clung to will not have gone to those who needed the most.

Even the younger workers are somehow mediocre workers, who got the jobs with those Vitamin B connections. They can't even spell names correctly, and yet they are supposed to advise people who are in dire need of jobs and social security. How can the blind lead the blind?

Pray that you don't fall into the hands of these mediocre employees. You will regret the day God created you as a human being. I know what I am talking about because I have been there. Even when you try to be respectful to them, they just ignore your presence, either directly or indirectly.

The first thing they ask is, "What brought you here?" The next thing you know, they grab the documents out of your hands before you can utter a word. And then they proceed with loud voices telling you, "Es ist festgelegt"(It is committed and written). When you hear these statements, it is certain that you will no longer be listened to. The next thing you will hear is, "Es tut mir leid" (I am sorry). And that marks the end of the conversation. No matter how urgent and serious the issue that brought you here was, you will be asked to come back the next day.

It is common these days to see security personnel around the job office workers. This is because these mediocre workers tend to raise tensions. Even when people are living on social benefits, they are not animals and do not deserve to be treated as such.

Instead of spending funds on security guards, why not spend the funds on preventive measures? For example, they could employ real professionals who try to listen to the clients and their needs. This would be much cheaper, and it would save everyone involved a lot of trouble. Sometimes people get frustrated, and fights between welfare workers and their clients break out. Most of these troubles could be averted, however, by employing qualified people, regardless of their race or religion.

Offering social and welfare benefits is not a bad idea at all. But it is a mistake to think these benefits can solve the problems of those living on them. When people use welfare as a way of life, rather than a boost to get through difficult times, the benefits actually worsen the situation over the course of time. You cannot suppress people's ambitions or dreams with welfare offers.

They might be receiving welfare benefits because they believe that's the best they can get, but inwardly, there is a vacuum of hopelessness and frustration. This can, at times, be reflected on the outside in the form of mental disorders and aggression.

People living on Hartz IV benefits, most of whom are foreigners and their children, are somewhat alienated from the mainstream society. They tend to keep to themselves because, if a German becomes aware you are receiving benefits, he or she distances him or herself from you, either indirectly or directly, as if you are suffering from a contagious disease.

Welfare recipients are often isolated socially, from neighbors, friends, and even some family members. Once people know you are receiving benefits, every time they see you, they talk about their jobs and money, knowing full well you are not in the position to join in on the conversation. So the people living on social benefits avoid people who are employed, and they are constantly in need of money.

It is a system that, if used as a short-term boost is good for people. But if the situation continues for a longer term, it turns humans into dogs. A dog may have its own teeth to bite, but human beings cultivated dogs to be dependent animals, to serve their own purpose.

A dog can never fend for itself, but humans are not dogs and can never ever have anything in common with them. I know this might upset some animal lovers. Let's face it; animals cannot really be substitutes for humans as many have claimed.

The late King Rainier of Monaco once claimed he trusted animals more than humans. This might be true for the short term, but it isn't true for a longer term. The king was talking to human beings like himself and not to animals. You can teach a dog to fulfill different purposes, but a dog has no human language. We are divine because we come directly from the almighty creator.

Science has proven otherwise, on a temporary basis, but everything is linked to only one source, which still remains a mystery. And that's all right with humans. After all, if a man knows he is the owner of the sun or has the ability to turn off the sun as he pleases, he is going to use it to serve his own purpose and the purposes of those around him.

We are humans, and we all have our way of viewing and passing through the process of life. But it all ends in the same way, even when it ends well. Some are not so fortunate. The most certain thing about life is that it's all going to end one day.

10

HAVING ELABORATED ON THE DIFFICULTIES and the challenges migrants face in Germany, I will now try, in the next few chapters, to reflect on why people do leave their natural homelands to seek peace and prosperity in a completely foreign land, different from the one they have always known.

Migration is as old as humans themselves, and it is the ultimate results of desperation in the face of survival. People leave their countries, towns, villages, and cities for a number of reasons. Human beings are constantly striving to survive and to have peace; this is a natural human thing.

Humankind's various reasons for migrating could well fit into seven categories—war, hunger, fear, persecution by tyrants, anarchy and chaos, the desire to acquire knowledge, and the quest for a better life.

When the brothers of Joseph, "the dreamer" in the Bible, sold him to traders on their way to Egypt little did they know that he would be the one to rescue them all. They were indirectly securing their survival in an unfortunate but predestined manner.

"Lets' see what will become of his dreams," they challenged.

That was the beginning of long years of oppression of the Israelites at the hands of the Egyptians, long after the dreams had been fulfilled and many generations had passed.

Hunger was an issue here. People wanted to be fed to keep their bodies and souls together. There was a great famine in Israel at the time, and the head of the family, Joseph's father, heard that there was food in Egypt. So he sent his children to Egypt to get some food. In the process, the brothers who had sold Joseph accidentally found him. They didn't know him anymore. Through interpreting his dreams, he had been able to tell the then king of Egypt that famine and hunger were imminent. He advised the pharaoh to store food to sustain them through the famine years, which the pharaoh did.

When Joseph's brothers eventually arrived in Egypt, Joseph recognized them, but they did not recognize him. He was now a chief and was surrounded by bodyguards. He had been elevated in a foreign land. A man who had once been sold as a slave had become a master of his own right.

After a series of test to determine whether his brother were still wicked, he eventually broke the news to his brothers about who he was. In addition, he invited them all to move to Egypt in order to survive the famine in their homeland, and they where given the land of Goshen in Egypt.

Hunger is a good reason people leave their home countries for other lands. Why is there hunger in some parts of the world and abundance in others? From time to time, human beings need to be confronted with challenges in order for them to open up to their potential.

In Europe and in Asia, as well as on the American continent, harsh weather conditions gave people far more survival initiative than others possessed. Without a doubt the winter is a long, cold season. If you don't gather food and wood in summer, you will not survive the winter. So survival of the harsh conditions makes gathering and thinking about the future imperative.

Harsh conditions, coupled with Francis Bacon's theory of looking to nature for answers and challenging nature, ultimately led to the Industrial Revolution, thereby making it possible for food to be produced in abundance. This eradicated hunger completely in these parts of the world with harsh weather conditions.

*****

Consider also people like Martin Luther, who encouraged people to look within themselves for solutions. All are part of that unique force that indirectly helps to eradicate hunger in Europe. Once people have solved their immediate need and hunger is no longer an issue in the country or city they've migrated to, other obvious issues now arise and must be dealt with.

They must find education, housing, and clothing. On top of it all, they must embark on the integration processes in their newfound land. Human wants are insatiable. No matter where people are, they always find one or two things to think about and work toward. People naturally tend to remain close to their place of birth. But the need for survival has prompted people to migrate almost since the beginning of humanity's existence.

Man has always been a wanderer. He moves from place to place in search of what he doesn't have—what others may have. Naturally, he goes to the place where he feels he can get what he actually needs. This is exactly why there are migrants.

*****

Sadly enough, most of these migration factors are man-made. The use of force to acquire what others possess often leads to war. Wars cause people to fear for their safety and migrate elsewhere in search of security. They travel thousands of miles—on seas, through deserts, and over mountains. Those who are fortunate enough make it to a new country. Often they have false documents or false excuses when travelling by air (economic migrants). Sometimes necessities naturally warrant the need for migration, in which case, countries is need of people will ask migrants to come.

For example, after the wars in Europe, in particular the Second World War, there were labor shortages in Germany. The Germans actually needed migrations in order to fill out their labor force and rebuild their industries and factories, which where destroyed at that time.

People from all across Europe and the world came. There was enough work for all, and people were in dire need of jobs. So they all came, first the men and then the women and children.

Many came to Germany anticipating they would save enough money to go back to their countries, settle back in, and live their normal lives. Such is easier said than done. For example, the Portuguese, the Turkish, the Italians, and others all came with the sole intention of sending money home to their various countries and returning home after a few years. For many, those few years have now turned into two and three generations.

Many, like I said, are forced to move against their will because of government policies. Policies that see ethnic or religious minorities as problems, in turn, lead to more wars and displacements, once again making migrations necessary.

The ethnic wars in Rwanda between the Tutsis and the Hutus that claimed millions of lives, the Holocaust in Europe that saw the deaths of more than six millions Jews, and the wars in former Yugoslavia that also saw the deaths of thousands all spread the migrating cancer in humans.

It may have been said after the Second World War that never again will there be war in Europe, but *never* is a word that humans rarely respect or take seriously. There need only be a little spark, and then you'll see human beings making exactly the mistakes all over again.

There is a place in the Bible—I think it was in the Old Testament—where God regretted ever having created man. On the upside, he allowed us to keep living, but at what price? He has since withdrawn his attention from humanity because the intent of humankind's heart is wickedness. We don't learn from our mistakes.

People do everything in their power to get a free ride off the sweat of the others, with the sole intention of being praised and honored.

***

Most migrants in Europe are economic migrants. They are escaping poverty in their various countries of origin, sometimes as a result of war. In other cases around the world, bad government policies and corruption are the causes of poverty, especially on the African continent.

I am convinced, that if there is total wars on corruptions on the African continents, like the one President Buhari of Nigeria has initiated, in no few years there is going to be few Africans, on the street of Berlin, Paris etc. Oppression, both internally and externally, are actually responsible for many failed states in Africa.

Very few people actually know the roots of African poverty and the mishaps that have befallen the continent. We always see the bigger picture, of children suffering from malnutrition, wars, and Ebola. We see, broadcasted over the media, dilapidated infrastructures; vast, arable, uncultivated lands; hunger and drought; and all sorts of negative news.

These are all true. But what are the reasons for these tragedies? Has anyone out there tried to understand why all these things are happening on the African continent? I try to explain it, as an African and as a Nigerian and as a German (a paper one).

I moved to Germany about two decades ago from Benin in southwestern Nigeria, after my secondary education. I was lucky to have a father who was keen on educating his children at all cost, and by all means possible.

I remember him telling his wives that he had no money for food for one month because he had just remitted money to his eldest son in Australia, who was studying at a university there. This was during the seventies, and the naira had great value.

My movement to Germany was sparked by the fact that, toward the middle of the eighties, things started changing for the worse. We had two military coups within two years. That was followed by the devaluation of the naira, structural adjustment programs, and austerity measures. All these—the changing of the naira notes, the changing of police uniforms, the creation of more states out of the nineteen states that existed at that time—were policies aiming nowhere. Today, we have more than thirty states, and all of the changes, including their creation are components of the driving force behind the poverty level in Nigeria today.

In addition, we have corruption that flows like rains pouring onto fields, like a running river eager to join the ocean, and like a bird that knows no borders and requires no visa to fly anywhere.

Only in Nigeria do politicians use oil wells as gifts for friends and relatives. A national wealth as a gift for friends? That's normal in Nigeria. I remember going to the passport office to have my passport made. The immigrations officer explained my options. To get a passport that day would cost me 2,000 naira. An express passport, which would take weeks to arrive, was 1,500 naira. For 500 naira, no time frame was given. Nor was there a guarantee that you'd ever get your passport. People where desperate, so they took the first and the second options.

Of the extra "fees", nothing went to the government. Yet the employees in the passport office expect to be paid their monthly salaries.

Who can blame them when the corruption comes from the top? The bottom might as well follow suit. Even when they give these fees to the government, in truth, one person steals all the money. In 2013, for example, the head of the police took the pension of the entire police force of the federation, worth billions of naira. He was fined only three million naira.

These are all factors that, when combined, render a state a backward state, or a failed state. When young, ambitious people no longer have opportunities in their own systems, the end result is that they will look elsewhere for their survival. Even when people have heard in the news there's a crisis in Europe, they are still determined to try and get to Lampedusa. I heard one person says "I'd rather die trying to get to Europe than meet my death after suffering in Nigeria, where those who have the cash make the laws. We don't need any laws in Nigeria. The politicians themselves *are* the laws of the land."

When Buhari, Nigeria's current president, was campaigning, everyone was saying he was going nowhere. I even read news story reporting that a prominent clergyman had said he would "open the gate of hell" for anyone who was against the incumbent government of Goodluck. That's an example of how impoverished the populace of Nigeria has become—a mortal person telling his own fellow human beings that he knows hell.

The situation reminds me of the early ages in Europe, when people were forgiven their sins if they paid money to clergyman and the church. Many opposition politicians, when they discovered that the election of Buhari was imminent, started switching sides, going to Buhari's party. They made this shift not on behalf of the common man, but to continue looting of the state and robbing the people of their fair opportunities to share in the national wealth of the state.

***

The refugees in Lampedusa are primarily Nigerians. They are not even Somalis or Ethiopians. Those war-devastated people don't even have the resources to pay the traffickers to take them there.

Once they get to Italy, the refugees come to understand that their suffering has only just begun, only now it'll take place in a different environment. You can find some on the beaches selling glasses or belts or shoes or just hanging around supermarkets to help customers push their shopping carts. They call it "shoroti," and we call them the "puree boys." Now tell me, is there any sense in all of this? Is there any justification that will explain why refugees should have to turn to literally begging on the streets of Venice, Rome, or Padova?

Let me explain some of the questions that need to be answered. Those traffickers are only a fraction of the problem. Most Nigerians who travel by sea are peasants without real resources but desperate to leave the country for one reason or another. For the most part, it's economic issues that push people to desperation.

Some of the women are deceived—promised they will be working as nannies in Europe and that they'll be able to send money home to their families. The traffickers charge exorbitant prices, which must be paid within a fixed period of time and sometimes earlier.

The traffickers, most of whom themselves reside in Europe, do the paperwork, which involves approximately six thousand dollars (for those travelling by air). The sea route is much, more cheaper. The women are made to pay up to fifty thousand dollars. Take a look at these figures. Even if these women should succeed in entering Europe and landing employment as nannies, raising the amount they are forced to pay will take more than fifteen or even twenty years.

The hidden agenda is simple but terrible. These women are unknowingly signing on for prostitution. In order to calm keep the girls' parents calm, the parents are told that their daughters will be getting nanny jobs. The girls are made to swear oaths in the presence of little gods should they default on what they supposedly owe the traffickers. These rituals sometimes involve the taking of the girls' private hairs or their fingernails. All of this is done to create an atmosphere of fear. The women are then manipulated and exploited mercilessly.

Once they get to Europe, the women are now concerned with paying their traffickers, also called "madams" or "sisters." It typically takes four years to pay back these "fees." On some occasions, when it looks like a woman may be able to pay the amount within a shorter period of time, the madams now inflate the price. It is an unimaginable story, but it is real.

***

The boat people of Lampedusa traveled a long way, sometimes to Abidjan, the Ivorian capital. From there, those who had the financial backings would travel by air to Paris. Those who did not would travel, sometimes through the desert to Mali and sometimes to Morocco. Next, they would find their way to Libya, and then they would take the sea route to Italy.

Meanwhile the journey through the desert is a dangerous undertaking. Travelers risk being robbed, beaten, or even killed by those involve in organ trafficking.

There is a center in Libya where these immigrants are detained. Some are there for two years waiting to join the ships bound for Europe. Some are even impregnated while there at the waiting camps, and the conditions there are devastating.

These situations happen because many do not want to go back home. They wouldn't know where to start with their lives, having sold all they have, perhaps their small furniture business or refrigeration business, for example, or having borrowed money from neighbors, friends, and relatives. Many are also escaping the wrath of rival gangs or cults. A wide range of socioeconomic challenges is involved when it comes to those trying to make it to Europe.

A chain of exploiters is preying on the desperation of people trying to escape poverty. This is not caused by his holiness but by humans, who through chance, greed, and paper empires control a whole country and all that is within it.

These migrants are paying a high price for life. They move from village to village, from town to town, from city to city, and then from country to country in the search of a better life—a dream that might be fulfilled. Sadly, in most cases, all that remains is shattered dreams.

***

The seas and oceans are calm.
He doesn't go to human beings,
Humans go to the seas and oceans
In search of goodies.

But the seas and oceans do not sell;
Humans do.
Children of old, why the troubles with the seas and oceans?
We are in search of better lives and goodies.
But the better lives you are seeking lie within you.
Why the risks and deaths?
The seas and oceans are weeping
Because they do not have the means of ever rescuing you.

If you dare swim,
They do not have the power over things they were meant to do.
To watch you go down,
Down and drown. That's the price.

***

The whole world is sad over the drowning of some three hundred migrants in seas. How about those whose deaths are not being reported, those who the rescue teams have not been able to locate? Where is the common sense? By what logic might anyone conclude that only three hundred have lost their lives while trying to make it to Europe?

11

THE EUROPEAN UNION HELD AN emergency meeting in Brussels to address the migrant crisis—a crisis that involves so many risking their very lives to make it to Europe. Their conclusion was to send more people on the high seas with high-tech equipment.

These measures support the companies apparently doing the job of securing the high seas against human traffickers. This does not address the problem of human beings being willing to risk death to try to make it to Europe. Those who do make it to dry land are still haunted by the problems and the challenges that brought them to Europe in the first place. These problems and challenges are deeply rooted in the societies they came from, mostly in the Middle East and Africa, where the sun shines on the very few, while most have never even heard of the word *sun*, let alone felt its rays.

It is a world that is deeply rooted in ethnic and religious sentiments used by the very few to enrich themselves and their associates, at the detriment of large populations who can barely make end meets. In various regions, these religious and ethnic sentiments, crowned with corruptions and inefficiencies, lead to disconnection between the people and the ruling class. This, in turn, leads to anarchy and wars and the desperation that fuels attempts to flee toward safe havens in Europe. It is this desperation that traffickers are you preying on.

They are making huge sums out of the chaotic situations prompted, in the first place, by various regimes and governments.

In Nigeria, for example, about three hundred different languages are spoken, most commonly Yoruba, Ibo, and Hausa. And so too are there three hundred ways of life. But we all have—or have had since the nation's independence in 1960—a common problem: There has never being any clear direction on how the nation should move forward after the British left.

The resulting confusion has created loopholes for people who think they are wise to play their ethnic cards for the sole purpose of self-gain, throwing the entire nation into chaos. The chaos has given way to no one being held accountable for anything, and that eventually paved the way for corruptions that have eaten deeply into society. The corruption is so great that there is even a coded term to describe a common scam—you might have heard of it by now. The 419 scam refers to crimes perpetrated by crooks of the highest order—thieves who fraud small-time "investors" out of money by way of fraudulent promises.

Corruption is the second unofficial anthem of Nigeria. Everyone dances and sings along with its tune. Even those who appear to be fighting against it are indirectly involved, or at least understand the lyrics of corruption. And they are bound to sing it if there is no one watching.

From the top to the bottom, Nigeria is saturated with corruption. There is no sense of responsibility anywhere. When the government of the day is left, all the politicians, some of the traditional leaders, and clergymen who are pretending to be men sent by God dance the left. When the government of the day is right, they all dance to the right.

When Buhari won the elections in Nigeria, everybody started declaring they were members of the APC, his party. They flocked in huge numbers to the victorious party. That's tradition in Nigeria. What's key to note here is that these "leaders" have no clear vision for the country. They are there to rape the country and the masses and, above all, to inflict pains on the people of the country by introducing and supporting lawlessness.

***

Nigeria's leaders encourage and support clergymen, and those pastors pose with them. They give them gifts and contracts that are never executed but paid for. In return, they go home with the confidence that they are backed by men of God.

The men of God, meanwhile, tell their congregations to be upright and not demand their rights, promising that God will avenge them and saying that their home is in heaven.

The trouble with this type of preaching is that the clergymen themselves live in villas and palaces. Some even possess private jets fuelled by politicians, and then they say that God gave them their wealth. Meanwhile, the members of the churches they head can't even afford three square meals a day. The parishioners of these churches wear torn clothes and broken shoes, and they go to the church almost seven days of the week. Some even become what is termed "prayer warriors." These people fast and pray. Some even attempt to fast forty days and forty nights like Jesus Christ. Yet the situation is deteriorating on a daily basis.

This reminds me of the "*ablass*" in Germany, whereby you can commit as many sins and atrocities in a year as you want and then go to the church and pay some money. In return, the clergyman will pray for you, and all your sins will be automatically forgiven.

Science is based on facts and experiments, which are probable. Religion is a mystery, based on invincible theories. Religions like these equate themselves with truth and love. But they are far from it, for man can manipulate them to suit his own agenda, crowned with greed.

I once heard a popular musician in Nigeria say that religion is politics, and politics on its own is based on the theory of bias. Its clear tenets are the suppression and oppression of human beings by those who are opportune enough to be elected to positions of authority.

***

The Supremacy Act in England, for example, was made so that the Church of England would be independent from the church in Rome. King Henry VIII was elected the head of the Church of England so that England would be independent from continental Europe, religiously and politically. While this may be true, the king's other motivation was that he never liked criticism. He was once criticized by the pope for being ruthless to women—divorcing wives and having affairs with women he was not married with.

He was thrown out of the church. He said, "Fine. Throw me out. The Church of England will go with me." Now tell me where was anything about the rules of God or Jesus mentioned in all of this?

These days in Nigeria, churches are like rice and sand, more so now that some churches are being banned because of noise pollution. My God, go to Lagos at 5:00 a.m., and you'll hear different noise from different angles, especially people praying and shouting in the name of Jesus Christ.

***

The refugee problems in Europe are man-made and not of God. The refugees are coming in high numbers, with the hope of having and maintaining a better life and a better future for their children and themselves. But these hopes are all but false because very few of them do have a better life, and their children are still being regarded as *Ausländer* (foreigners). For most part, they have the status of second-class citizens, even when they were born and raised in Europe. Once you are foreign, you are automatically denied the full rewards for your performances and hard work, regardless of what you do to sustain life.

Mixed race children are regarded as *"negerkinder,"* but these children are growing in numbers, and they are very well ahead of their parents in terms of the social problems attached to their skin colors or appearance.

Many are determined to push beyond boundaries and to become successful in life. However, the barriers and limitations in their way are a huge challenge that must be overcome now and not tomorrow.

These young people face many frustrating situations. For example, even if they work hard and make good grades, someone who is german without good grades may be considered for employment opportunities before them. They are often not taken seriously. That's a very frustrating thing for any human being to deal with.

***

The German social system is embodied in the country's constitution and cannot be changed easily. It is one of the best in the world, especially when it comes to the health care delivery systems. Otto Bismarck was well ahead of time when he introduced the health systems alongside the social system. These systems mean that everyone who is legally recognized by the State should be given the right to medical attention.

If there is anything in Germany that doesn't discriminate based on origin, race, or religion, it's probably the health systems. I once worked with the German Red Cross in the ambulance sections. I can confirm based on personal experience, both in that work and in living for over two decades in Germany, that there is little or no real difference between an asylum seeker and a "higher-class" person like, say, a medical doctor.

I remember taking a sick woman to the hospital. She had been staying at a refugee camp in a southern German city called Freiburg, a border city with Switzerland and France. The only thing that was asked of her at the hospital was her identity. Upon determining she was a refugee, the social office arranged to take care of all the bills, and she was immediately taken to the appropriate unit of the hospital.

Even those who feel they need private health insurances do not really have different experiences with health care. They are, perhaps, talked to by a professional throughout the experience, or they get single rooms to themselves while in the hospital. But the hospital is no hotel and should not be treated as such. Hospitals do need to be built according to certain standards so that they help in the healing process, which, with all the conformity, is the case in Germany.

If the approach in the health care system were transferred to other areas, like employment and other opportunities for migrants and foreigners, it is unlikely anyone would ever complain about not being integrated.

12

Sadly enough, the integration of foreigners will begin to unfold in about twenty to fifty years time in Germany. By then, though, there will no longer be anyone to stay and talk about the integration. Even as I write, a trend of empty buildings and apartments has already started in the eastern and some western parts of Germany.

The ripple effects of people living longer, combined with the demographic changes that are happening everywhere have also arrive in Germany. Politicians try to play these trends down, but the effects are already being felt in many communities in Germany. Kindergarten closures due to lack of children are one such occurrence. Among the reasons for this are the constant movement of people of childbearing age to bigger cities in search of jobs and women having children later in life. All of this makes it difficult to "keep Germany only for the Germans. The generations contract (*generationen vertrag*)—the system by which the old take care of the young and then the young take care of the old—is at the blink of collapse. Unless real, honest integration methods are set in place and enlightenment campaigns are utilized, Germany will be unable to sustain its course as a united country.

I once read that humans don't change. I believe people do change, but the sacrifices involved are a bone of contention. It is far cheaper to initiate a change than it is to wait and delay change. Of course, we all know the price of change. Moving from one's home or potential to somewhere new when it's too late to implement change is far more expensive, with little or no room for negotiation.

Germany accepts more refugees than does any other European country. The problem is, what becomes of those refugees and migrants? Are they able to move on with their lives? Are they given the necessary tools to become productive members of the society they live in? Are they integrated? Are they even accepted? To all these questions, I have only one answer—no.

Let's look at two more questions about refugees living in Germany: What have their lives and achievements been in the past, say, ten years? What will their future be?

In order to answer those questions in a positive manner, much needs to be done. One cannot change the older generation's mind-set. We can, however, try to influence the next generation's mind-set. We can initiate programs that show people the realities of the current system and teach them the true meaning of full integration.

The Germans are a prosperous people, but prosperity needs continuity and sustainability. In order for this prosperity to continue, Germany needs more migrants and to fully explore the potential of those migrants. With one of the lowest birthrates of the industrialized nations, Germany needs migrations and integration in order to support her social system and secure her future.

It would be a grievous mistake not to rethink the current position in regard to the proper integration of migrants. This month alone more than six hundred thousand migrants have crossed the Mediterranean to Greece en route to Germany. They are coming from places like Syria, Ethiopia, and Iraq. These developments are a burden on the system. But the advantages of such massive migrations should not be underestimated.

***

Furthermore, the migrants who are already in the country should never be confined to job centers (social welfare centers). In these spaces, people's livelihoods are determined by social welfare workers who are ill equipped to take on the needs of these individuals.

I will describe people living on the benefits received through the welfare benefits offices called job centers thusly:

> People waiting in silence, not knowing what comes next,
> People with ideas and dreams—
> Some lost in daydreams, some with sad faces, some in deep thought,
> Some with heads directed to the earth, seeking answers to questions
> That may never be answered.
> Some have hopes and fears about the future; some have lost faith in themselves.
> Some are old and weak, wishing the next hour would be their last.
> Some failed to plan; others planned but failed.
> I saw a woman, trying to bury her face in the wake of frustrations
> In the newspaper open before her.
> You can see clearly she is not reading
> For comfort but for frustrations.
> All these people have one thing in common—
> They are all at the job center.

***

People who happen to be on this welfare scheme are the lowest on the ladder of a social society—A society that is supposedly based on "one for all, all for one." They are people with long histories of unemployment and little or no hope of ever again gaining sustainable long-term employment.

Many are foreigners. In fact, 90 percent are either foreign born or have migration backgrounds. They are people like me, who left their homelands in search of greener pastures and a future that is better future than the prospects most of them have ever know.

But these job centers are capitulation stations—where foreigners and migrant finally surrender their hopes for better lives for themselves and their families.

At these welfare benefits offices, people are treated like files, not human beings. I can say this because I have been a part of the system for quite. And I am thoroughly convinced that many people feel the same way I do. There are also some Germans who are in the system, but they are very few, and among them, many are alcoholics.

Many of the job center employees are ill equipped to entertain the challenges involved in dealing with people with frustrations and anger—the direct results of difficult in lengthy periods of unemployment. They do not even take the time to listen carefully to their clients, and their answers are, most of the time, delivered in sarcastic tones.

***

Recently, I went to the job center to inform my job adviser of my prospects of securing employment in a southern city called Stuttgart. His response, not surprisingly, was skepticism. The first thing he asked me was whether the company that wanted to employ me was German? I said it was. "Is the person in charge German?" he asked next, noting that the man's name wasn't German. I explained that that was because the person in question was of Moroccan descent.

I was upset with this line of questioning, but it was nothing new to me.

He then went further, saying that the job center did not support my quest to have that kind of a job. He added that he would first discuss the situation with his team leader. It was the most devastating moment of all my experiences in Germany.

I was not willing to accept no for an answer. The company in question had promised to train me for six weeks—at its own cost. The only expenses the company would not be responsible for were my room and board during the six-week period.

I had gone to the job center to seek help with those expenses, and here was someone telling me that wasn't going to happen. I was 100 percent certain that it was within the purview of the job center to handle such costs. After all, the training would enhance the process of my finding employed again.

I immediately sent an e-mail to the head of my job adviser's department, explaining my situation and how badly I needed a job. I could not afford to be living on social and unemployment benefits for the rest of my life when I was mentally and physically fit to carry out full-time employment.

It was after my e-mail that I met the very kind (and gorgeous) Mrs. Arends, a woman I once described as "too good for this world." I say this because of the way she has extended herself on behalf of the unemployed and especially her wonderful human understanding, which goes beyond what we can see and absorb but directly into the components that makes us human. She can actually communicate with one's soul.

Upon receiving the e-mail, Mrs. Arends called to ask what the matter was. I explained everything to her. She was happy to hear that I would be getting a job soon and told me to be patient. She would discuss the issue with my job adviser.

The next day, my job adviser called and asked me to come to his office in the afternoon. This time, he was friendly, but he maintained a great deal of reservations. I observed that he had changed his opinion and attitude slightly, but I sensed that, underneath it at all, he was questioning, why is this guy leaving the job center?

When I first arrived, he told me he was deeply sorry for his attitude toward me the previous day before. He had not been well informed about the prospects of my getting the upkeep money during the six-week training period.

I told him that I was thinking about others—those who might not be as fortunate as I am to understand and write the German language and who had been jobless for too long. I told him that his attitude toward me was not encouraging at all and that, even if he did not know what to do or understand the process, he must learn to listen to the facts and statements of the people he was intended to help and tried to grasp the realities of their situations. I explained that many people at the job centers had not chosen that path on their own. Rather, situations had chosen it for many of the people he advised. Hence they were frustrated by the situation they found themselves in.

Moving out of the system takes a lot of courage on the part of the person involved. It also requires the support of his or her job adviser. For the job adviser to reject outright the proposal for a job prospects on the part of the clients is frustrating.

***

There is nothing more frustrating for a man with the appropriate sense of humanity than to wake up in the morning not knowing where to go, not able to take care of his family.

The social system in Germany is a "ticking time bomb" because it has made human beings dependent on the state for virtually everything—from household utensils to health care and education.

These are all good social products, but the nature of humankind makes us desire to stand on our own and be self-reliant. That's what people are supposed to do—not receive social handouts that rape a man of his pride, his vigor, and his natural inclination to gather and build.

Social handouts are good on a short-term basis, but on a long-term basis, they are dangerous and unsustainable. Being a long term recipient causes one stop thinking about the future. He or she is restricted to the handouts, like a dog that barks but is completely dependent on its owner for survival.

Sadly enough, it is mostly foreigners and their children who are recipients of these social handouts, along with a few Germans who are alcoholics or are sick in one way or the other.

Why is it mostly foreigners who are recipients of these social handouts? The reasons are to be found in the job markets, in schools, and in homes and social gatherings.

The enabling environments are restricted and highly controlled by the society, not the government.

***

The government can initiate and put in place measures to help properly integrate foreigners properly, but those charged with executing these measures are confined to the theory "German first." This theory undermines the potentials and ability of anyone who is not of German descent.

It is not common to see anyone who is not of German origin wearing nice suits to his place of work in Germany. Immigrants and their children—even the third and fourth generations—are confined to mediocre jobs like cleaning, driving, and collecting garbage. They work as delivery boys (*bote*) in big offices, kitchen cleaners, hotels bed dressers, bread sellers, and so on—jobs that Germans shy away from.

The problem with these jobs is they are unskilled, and unskilled jobs earn low wages. As a result, these forced "unskilled" workers are rendered dependent on these services jobs for the rest of their lives, unable to take the steps necessary to occupy any meaningful positions, even in the companies they were before.

They work and work until they get their pensions, which are not enough to pay their house rents. Then they resort to the aid of the state to help them cover the expense of their livelihood.

I referred to these people as *forced "unskilled" workers* because most of them would have achieved better things and aims in lives if they had ever been given the slightest opportunity. A society should be fair enough to reward those willing to make a difference—to give everyone an equal opportunity to do so, rather then simply packing everyone who is not of full German origin or into the same bucket and pretending all is okay.

Germany lacks skilled workers today, in part due to this mentality of "German first." Every society has this notion of protecting the interest of its citizens first. This is normal and natural, but it becomes abnormal when there is a bias that leads to denying someone outright because he or she doesn't look German or posses a German name, like Koch, Müller, Schwarzkopf, or Scholz.

***

The United States of America is a dominant country in the world today because of its notion that all men are created equal and endowed with inalienable rights. These are not just words. They are declarations that speak to humanity as a whole—declarations that, if applied, could lift any nation to whatever heights it wishes to achieve.

The United States was not built around peace and prosperity. It was built around the above declarations. And it was built around the beliefs that, if you try hard enough, one day, you will succeed and that everyone should be given the opportunity of his or her lifetime. This is what the United States has believed in and has worked toward until now. There is no way the country is going to take a second place in the world, not even for the next thousand years.

There are emerging nations that want to take over the US position. Their chances are good, except for the fact that they lack substance. Anything that lacks substance is like a sperm without a head—unable to achieve its aims and objectives.

The opportunities extended to people in the United States enable those with creative abilities to move from dishwashers to billionaires. This can never happen elsewhere because other systems are noninclusive.

***

The German system is exclusive, and there are millions of people in this country who would have conceived good ideas and brought forth marvelous innovations, but they were cut off before they ever had happy opportunity to begin.

The government knows very well that the situation with foreigners and migrants is not in good shape. What it doesn't know is exactly how to sell the idea of changing the contributing structures. After all, the German people have, until now enjoyed a great deal of privileges by influencing, directly or indirectly, the policies of the government. This is true of real democracy. Sometimes, though, a government must put in place policies that, while they might not be popular with all her citizens, will determine the destiny of her people.

For example, Abraham Lincoln went to war to keep the union together. Little did anyone knew at the time that such forced unity was going to be beneficial to all—a contributing factor that would ensure the United States of America's position as the greatest nation on earth in modern times.

The first movable car was built in Germany in 1886 by Gottlieb Daimler. The vehicle had about 1.1 ps (metric horsepower). It was the first in the world at the time. Why is the United States leading the car industries? The answer is simple. The United States allows more room for innovations than does any other country—encouraging the potential in almost anything, from humans to animals.

The US systems are not concerned about who you are but about what you can offer, where your potential lies, and how they can help you think better. They are not concerned about what was but about what will be.

The civil wars in America started in Manassas in Virginia. Today, there is a shopping mall right where the wars started. The Europeans, on the other hand, are too busy with things of the past—too caught up with wars fought and won and lost and with the suffering that withered the continent some seventy years ago. It was declared, "Never again"—that there would never again be wars in Europe. But what happened in the nineties when Europe saw the Bosnian War?

I know some critics will be ready to say that the people in the Balkans or in the Caucasus are not Europeans. The Russians called the people of Chechnya "blacks." Statements like these are all said to buy time. But how much can a man buy out time? Time is like the stars in the sky. Although they're millions of miles away from the earth, they can be seen with the bare eyes when the night falls. The same is true of truth.

Like the stars in the sky, the truth can never be hidden. It is seen everywhere by everyone. The Chechnyans are not blacks, and neither the Caucasus nor the Balkans are not Africa. Both are on the European continent, no matter how hard anyone tries to dismiss them or carve them out.

The United States is always looking forward, rarely concerned about the past. That's why her people have built shopping malls on the places where the civil war started. In Europe, a statue of Jesus Christ would have been erected, for generations to see. Preserving cultural heritage is good, but too much of anything is bad. The German culture clings too much to the past.

***

Germany exports nearly 50 percent of her GDP, mostly to Europeans countries, with very little consumed at home. Why is little being consumed at home? Because the people are not financially buoyant enough to have the purchasing power to consume more.

The social systems that exist here in Germany are based on the concept "one for all, all for one." However, the current biased, invincible segregation of foreigners and their children disregard that principles. It is a social problem that urgently needs recognition and solutions. Instead, it is being swept under the carpet in all aspect of life.

The world has changed a great deal in the past twenty years times, and it will continue to change. Nothing can change times from changing. Powers have shifted in the order running the world. Europe is struggling with its position in the world. Asia has taken over Europe, with the rise of China; the already established Japan; and India, with its growing population and innovations.

The engine of Europe is Germany, seconded by France. While France has long recognized the importance of integrating immigrants, Germany is reluctant to take the opportunity of making use of her population, which is the largest in Europe.

I think about young people who are not being given the opportunity to prove themselves, about the young people who are willing but not accepted, about the talents wasted. I think about the destiny of the common good and about how, for so many theirs is already determined by the society they where born into. I think about people, mostly foreigners, running their accounts and budgets on overdrafts and the excessive interest rates set by the banks and about the growing numbers of unemployed migrants and their families seeking unemployment benefits. Then I try to look through the eyes of a dead man, lying still with no breath, and I ask the question, what he would have done differently?

***

The German society is an aging society, with very low birthrates— among the lowest in Europe. It is only through proper integration and absorption of foreigners that the living standards and the continuity of this land will be guaranteed.

People of color or immigrants, no matter how long they have lived in Germany or for how many generations their families have been a part of this society, are still being treated as foreigners and are constantly denied opportunities that would enable them to move forward and realize their dreams.

All human beings, no matter where they were born or the color of their skins, have potential. The fact that we are human beings automatically endows us with wonderful, God-given potential. Unfortunately, this truth is recognized by some while being completely ignore or subdued by others. The latter is sadly the case in Germany. The potential placed within each of us by the almighty God can never be subdued. A society that does not integrate cannot innovate.

Foreigners in Germany have all too often succumbed to a paralyzing realization: "If I succeed in learning a profession, I cannot succeed in fully realizing my dreams." In other words, no matter how hard they try, they will never be accepted in the society they belong to but are not part of.

The result is clear—you have more people working low-wage, "mediocre" jobs than professionals, more school dropouts, and more poverty among foreigners than you have among their ethnic German counterparts. The reason there has not been increase in crime rates here is the social welfare system. This system has kept society flowing peacefully. But for how long can a nonintegrated society stand in its old ways and think, "We are mastering our society"?

13

For anyone to think that Germany is not an immigrant nation is a horrible mistake that must be amended. This nation is an immigrant nation in full. However, institutional and societal isolations of those not deemed Germans by name, color, religion, and the like are ongoing. That's the simple truth.

There may be people in drowning boats still dreaming of "homogenous societies." And there may be people who say, "If you don't like living here, then leave." Regardless of the legitimacy of these attitudes, how can you tell a child who was born and raised here he or she doesn't have the right to opportunities because of his or her skin color, religion, or ethnic background? How can you tell a little black girl or boy born and raised in Germany or a Turkish youth or a Palestinian refugee that he or she can never be employed by the police force or become a judge in the justice departments? How can you explain to these people that, if they so much as try to do so, they will be cut off with a force as great as a hurricane pounding a city and leaving behind destruction, pains, and even death?

What we have in Germany reminds me of countries with caste systems, in which the family or the caste one comes from determines one's destiny. In some countries, there are those who are born slaves and remain slaves throughout their lives. They live like slaves, are treated like slaves, and die like slaves. They are even buried like slaves. The lives of these individuals are slavery.

While Germany might not be the same as these countries, the principle is almost the same. Your educational background is determined by your family's background.

Anyone who doubts that Germany, by all respects, is already an immigrant should visit a town called Bad Canstatt, a suburb of Stuttgart in Southern Germany. Go to a shopping mall called Carre, and there you'll find the true definition of being an immigrant or foreigner in Germany.

You will also observe the signs that a societal system is failing and what it looks like when a government tries desperately to hold onto old ways and keep its citizens calm, ensuring them they are living in the best place in the world. That maybe true for some, but it is certainly not the case for the common man or for foreigners, who are nothing but hamsters running on a wheel twenty-four hours a day, for their entire lifetimes.

The shopping mall is filled with foreigners—blacks, whites, Eastern Europeans, Arabs, Turks, Pakistanis, Indians, and more—all passing time. You can see on their faces that they are just trying to get by. They all have one thing in common—they are scraping by, existing on the minimum possible. In other words, living on social welfare benefits. Some are from families who are into their second and third generations of living this way.

"True Germans" here are few. You'll find them wearing clean police uniforms, chasing purported thieves or investigating shopliftings, you'll find them in the offices. The salespeople on the payments terminals are foreigners, happy to be employed in these positions, earning minimum wage (about nine euros per hour) and paying house rents of about seven hundred euros a month. Some have a child; others do not. Either way, do the math, and it's clear the salaries are barely enough to support existence.

You are also going to find poor older Germans or alcoholics, who have given up the struggle. As a result, the latter group does one thing—they drink in order to forget their frustrations with life. They were told for so long they had German names and were born Germans; they needed to do little to get more out of life than every other person who was not German. Thus, they were tied to a particular place of work without ever thinking of eventualities.

In life, nothing remains the same; all things change. When a company goes bankrupt, the Germans find it difficult to adjust and move on. They are consumed by old memories, so going to work in other company becomes a problem. They are afraid they won't be accepted. They are afraid their abilities and competency will be ruined by the people who do not like them. They are afraid they will be ignored by their new employer and colleagues. They wonder how long it will be before they have a say at their new place of work. Will their new colleagues ever accept their views on matters?

With all these thoughts and insecurities, some find it difficult to move on. Some may try, but others just give up hope.

***

It is not uncommon for a father to encourage his son or daughter to work in the same company where he was employed or encourage his child to take up his profession and, eventually take over his practice or business. Many parents are greatly disappointed if their children decide to pursue other professions.

While taking over ones parent's business is not a bad ideas, it does not encourage innovations. Young people are not encouraged to try to live what they believe in. Children are only subject to whatever rules are laid out before them, and any child acting outside the rules come even a little bit, is considered rude.

Once any child is considered rude by one teacher, in the case of schools, other teachers will never take the time to thoroughly investigate the child's character, preferring rather to simply support their colleague by agreeing that the child is rude.

The case is much worse for children of color or for those with migrant backgrounds. I remember when my daughter was only two years old, she resisted going to a particular day care. She was always weeping and throwing herself to the ground every time her mother took her to that day care. Finally, I made a decisions to take her there and find out why.

I sat down and watched the children play, the body language of their tutors, and the way they interacted with the children. After that, I went to the manager of the complex and asked why she thought my daughter did not like coming to her day care.

She said she suspected my daughter's feelings related to the fact that we did not speak German with her at home. Because of this, the manager told me, she did not fully understand the playing rules. She suggested that my daughter's mother and I take her to the doctor and, thereafter, to place where she could learn German.

I thought I was dreaming to hear these accusations, but then I knew already what this was all about. Migrant children were not really welcomed in places of learning. It's not that they weren't welcomed physically. Rather, the integrations we all need as humans to succeed in life we're not present in places of learning. This is a subject I would love to see you taken under discussion. After all, the destinies of the countless wonderful children are at stake. Far too many never have the opportunity to prove their cases. The denials start as early as three years old.

Try to understand the situations of these children (and adults) who came to this land, for one reason or another, in search of better lives and are told as soon as they arrive, directly or indirectly, that they will never be useful or considered an integral part of the society they have joined.

A child is not responsible for who his or her parents are. If that was the case, the poor would never have children of their own.

***

I took my daughter away from the day care and enrolled her in a new one. Soon, she was telling me that she liked to go to days care. She brought me children's book and asked me to read them for her. She could count up to thirty. I never took her to the doctor or any language school.

This lesson meant a lot to me. It taught me about living in a society that limits migrants, automatically classifying them among its lowest ranks. All human beings, regardless of race, color, or gender can unlock their potentials, if only they are given the encouragements and opportunities to do so. The same fears Germans would have if they loose their jobs of life—these are exactly the fears society forces on migrants and their children by not taking them seriously and ignoring their views on matters.

Let's say, for example, you are a foreigner and you get into a discussion with a German. In this scenario, one or two other Germans are in the room but not taking part in the discussion. You will soon see in the German's face that he does not want to further the discussion. He will start glancing to the left or right to see if anyone else in the room is listening. If not, he'll change the subject matter or conclude with you abruptly. Or he'll simply start another discussion by asking the other German(s) about almost anything—all in an effort to divert the attention away from your conversations, which he now considers boring.

It takes time and interest to figure out this mentality, but in my more than twenty years of living here, I have figured out this is a normal occurrence.

Recently, I had a conversation with a German friend, in which I told her I was considering becoming a nurse and, thereafter, setting up an ambulance service in Nigeria. Even after I'd mentioned Nigeria, she replied, "Aber das in dein Heimatland" (But in your home country).

"Nein in Deutschland" (No, in Germany), I replied.

She told me that she didn't understand my German language anymore.

She did not believe it possible for a foreigner or black man like me to have an ambulance service in Germany. This is just one example of the many kinds of setbacks foreigners experience on a daily basis here.

A friend once said, if you dream of becoming successful in life outside your own land of birth, you'd better not come to Germany. Here, you will be made to wash dishes, and cleaning toilets will become your profession. This is evident by the fact that anytime there is a job opening for, say a warehouse attendant or forklift driver, the employer is sure to get hundreds of people applying for the vacancy.

When there are job vacancies for engineers, doctors, computer engineers, biologist, and so on, there is a vacuum. Many jobs that require expertise are vacant because there's nobody to fill the empty spaces.

14

THERE ARE REASONS THAT GERMANY is facing a growing lack of professionals. In order for a country to survive, it needs to look first to its citizens before looking outside. The same is true for us as humans. Before we want to effect a change, we need to look within ourselves. Only then can we begin to make the various moves that best suit or answer our quest for almost anything.

Now there are young Germans who no longer want to be a part of this so-called generation's contracts. Explained in simple terms, those contracts require that the old take care of the children, and the children, when they are older, take care of the elderly. That's what the German pension system is all about, but there is a crack in the system now.

As I've said before, society does not want to change. However, the cost of making changing on our own will be much less than that of waiting until time forces us to change. The young Germans do their best to obtain knowledge at various universities. Thereafter, they simply find their way to other countries, where they feel they can open up their horizons and be fully rewarded for their services. This is the truth. The older generations always want full control over the younger generations and, thereby, don't create room for the necessary changes that human minds need to keep up with.

Many young Germans simply migrate to the United States, Australia, Canada, and even China. The Chinese have been able to recognize the effects of making their land attractive to foreigners and are doing their best to encourage it. The Germans, on the other hand, remain true to their old-fashioned ways. We are still at the top for the time being, but the competitors are not sleeping.

***

The other problem with the system is that Germans are very reluctant to see the potential in foreigners and their children, other than to make them dependent on the state to survive through destructive social handouts. This system simply groups all foreigners and migrants to particular a zone of accepting social welfare.

I used to work with a Lebanese citizen who came here in 1982. He told me that one of his sons, a mechanic, happened to team up with a close relative to purchase a two-bedroom flat, which they rented out. One day, his son made an announcement that they were looking for a renter for the flat. Because Freiburg, where the flat was located, is a university town, a lot of people, all Germans, wanted to rent the flat for their children who were just beginning their studies in Freiburg.

My colleague's son went to make the necessary contract arrangements. One of the parents approached his son and asked, "Are you really the owner of this apartment? Or are you working here?" (The parent was asking whether he was there cleaning the apartments. Oh, you need to hear terms used to describe foreigners.)

He simply responded that he was, indeed, the owner and asked if the father had a problem with that. You see, Germans have a certain perception of who foreigners and migrants are. They see them as people who don't understanding the language, aren't educated, are willing to take everything thrown at them, and are existing but not living.

Once you do not fit into any of the above categories, they become suspicious and begin with their "sarcastic inquisitiveness." They comment on how good your German is, ask how long you have been in Germany, and enquire if you plan to go back to your country.

It isn't that they are actually interested in all of that stuff. They are looking for clues about whether you have any dreams and, if so, how you intend to fulfill them (or more specifically, whether you intend to do so in Germany).

***

An average German professional cannot afford a very large house for himself. This is because, compared to their counterparts elsewhere, German professionals are paid peanuts. There's a massive brain drain. The low pay is one of the causes. Another is that Germany, according to some studies, is not an attractive land for experts because, a few years ago, the Germans wanted to give so-called green cards to foreign expatriates to help them in their computer branch. They were inviting expatriates from India and Malaysia.

One politician, referring to the experts from India, simply said, "Was weiss ein elefanten verkäufer über computer?" (What do elephant sellers know about computers?). Another said, "Kinder statt inder soll an der computer" (Children instead of Indians should be sitting on the computer.).

The list of such comments is long, but I want to focus more on the effects that such doubts in the competency of foreigners cause. And I want to point out that if anybody with a migrant background is to succeed and live a normal life in Germany, this doubt must cease to exist.

Germany is a land of inherited properties. People pass their properties from one generation to the next. This is normal human behavior. It becomes abnormal when people build their foundations on inherited properties. It becomes abnormal when people only visit their grandparents if they have some property to inherit in the future. (I'm not suggesting that all Germans only visit their grandparents if they have properties to share, but there is evidence of neglected old who do not have means.) It becomes abnormal when people build their foundations on inherited properties. If you do not have an inheritance, it is very difficult to own a house in Germany.

Innovation here in Germany has been sleeping for so long because the old are still in control of literally everything. The older generation believes they can do it much better, but things have changed now. When things change, people must change too. Otherwise, the price society will pay for not changing will be enormous.

***

Carre, the shopping mall I mentioned earlier, is a ghost town filled with people. I say this because people there simply walk by you, not quite living and almost like the living dead. It's as if they are moving only because of the inward mechanism God created to sustain life, so long as the breath continues.

Of these shopping malls visitors, some 70 percent are foreigners. They are either unemployed and living on welfare benefits, involved in prostitution, or wrapped up in the drug business. You will be surprised at what you are going to see, but it won't be the kind of surprise that's funny. Most of the people you'll encounter there are on their way either to jail at some point in future or to living their lives just like that, as burdens to the state. For now, the state can finance these welfare systems, but for how long will that be the case?

If 70 percent of migrant and foreign citizens, along with a large portion of the elderly, continue to live on welfare and be without employment to help finance the social state, and if the low birthrates remain as they are, the system will collapse. Then there will be a problem, not just for Germany alone but also for all of Europe and then the world at large.

***

People in Germany are afraid to make a move and fail, so they preach the sermon of security (*sicherheits*)—financial securities, that is. They don't want to make a move and wind up losing. Of course nobody wants to lose. But if there is no such thing as losing, how can there be any such thing as gaining?

If there is no such thing as death, how can there be life? The opportunities given to one person could be the key to rescuing an entire society. That's what the United States has been able to incorporate into her constitution and into the minds of her children, singing to them on a daily basis that they need to take the opportunities given to them and rise to the top. US citizens are encouraged to exploit opportunities to the fullest and take all of the benefits that come from them. There is nothing sweeter on earth to give human beings than the feelings that they are part of a large family—a family that is telling them they can work hard and be all they can be and want to be. Here in Germany, children are constantly reminded of their origins.

Turkish children are told they are "Deutsche mit migrationshintergrund" (Germans with migrant backgrounds). This is, more or less, a way of telling someone he or she is not German— you may have been born here, the expression says, but you are not *from* here. As a result, Turkish citizens try to organize their own structures, such as schools, banks, and insurance companies.

Turkish people would now prefer to deal with their own people, rather than deal with Germans. They now treat Germans with suspicion, just as has been done to them. They keep to themselves. But why are they closing their doors like this? The answers are simple. Human beings learn faster and more than any other animals. The problem with human beings is that they take time to study and evaluate properly and then apply what they have learned to the decisions they make.

With more than six hundred thousand migrants coming to Germany this year alone and an estimated two hundred thousand additional migrants predicted to arrive at the end of the year, the need for policy and societal change around the treatment of migrants and their children is imperative. Germany must to come to terms with the fact that her land is already an "immigrant land."

***

Without a doubt, every country will always strive hard to protect its territories against the influx of illegal immigrants. That's essential. But migration on its own is compatible with humanity and should be accepted as such by all people.

Recently, a friend visited me, along with his two daughters. I asked one of them what she would like to become when she grows up.

"A police officer," she replied.

My friend looked at me, and I looked at my girlfriend, and we all started laughing. We were laughing not because she had chosen the wrong profession but because we did not believe, for now, her choice was a possibility.

I was reminded of the little boy from Sudan who I'd seen in Boston. I thought of his confidence when he said he wanted to be a "cop" and was reminded of the promised dream in the United States of America.

I have no doubt that Germany, with all its resources, can one day accept people of different backgrounds the way they are and integrate them in honest terms. After all, no man is an island.

Likewise, no country is an island. Human movements and commerce ensures that is so. In spite of violent attacks on asylum seekers in recent times, I believe that the position of many Germans, especially younger Germans, on migrants is one of positivity. However, the country as a whole needs enlightenment, and the old fear that migrants will take away jobs meant for Germans must be torn down, as this is far from truth.

The refugee crisis in the world today was caused by humans. It is not a result of natural disasters such as hurricanes, earthquakes, or severe storms. Hence the refugee "problem" is of human nature.

A comprehensive and honest dialogue is required to alleviate the painful experiences of those who are running for their lives—from war and poverty and from corruption and mismanagement in their various countries.

Wars and destruction are not of God. Neither is poverty or disease. All of these tragedies are caused by human beings because of deeply rooted desires in human nature. All were born of humanity's compunction to manipulate others and the environment to satisfy individual desires.

Because these crises are caused by humans, only humans can solve them. We need no magic mirrors (which is good, since none exist anyway).

We are living in a world that is the only world we know as humans. Various religions have taught us that there is another one after this. They are all competing for clients. But who, among all of these voices, should we believe? Is there any justification for one individual telling another what to do in the name of religion? Who is any person to tell his fellow men the way they ought to live?

I believe God dwells in us all. Hence, we can be free like him. All we must do is obey a simple rule: Act toward others the way you would like them to act toward you. As simple as that rule is, it's very difficult to obey. We are all busy focusing on what would be and what should not be—things as intangible as promises of the existence of another world beyond this one. For now, we are here, and we should be concerned with what is now, particularly in relationship to how we accept and treat others.

I am a paper German. (Ich bin ein Papier Deutsche.)

We live in a very simple world, then we are surrounded, with challenges which must overcome. And we are tempted to believe, its a complex world. Life is as simple as breathing, if only we could recognize and cherish the beautifulness of life, as a passage endowed with mutual respects for one another, dignity for one another,then we are assured of a peaceful life, in our lives. Let your heart and soul guide you, in it is the power of love.